Understanding War

With the exception of Clausewitz, no reflective thinker has seriously engaged with the concept of war – with its persistent changeableness and the dominant direction of its changes.

The results of this failure are seen in the extreme logical weakness of most debates, during the last two centuries, on the possibility of eliminating war and, since 1945, on the possibility of eliminating nuclear weapons.

Orderly, clear and reflective, *Understanding War* develops two main theses, first, that the horrendous escalation of war's destructiveness in this century is primarily the result of the inherently cumulative character of war itself rather than of the application to war of recent science-based technologies; and second, that the irreversible destructiveness of nuclear weapons suggests how joint action by the superpowers could prevent their being used in any future war.

W. B. Gallie is Emeritus Professor of Political Science at the University of Cambridge. He has taught and written widely in philosophy, politics and the history of ideas – including military ideas – and saw over five years' military service in World War II.

POINTS OF CONFLICT

A new series from Routledge

The books in this series mark a new departure in academic publishing. Written by philosophers, or from a philosophical standpoint, their purpose is to probe beneath the shibboleths of day-to-day debate and controversy on important social and political topics. Common to all the authors is a view of the importance of the analytical skills of the professional thinker in reaching decisions on the large issues of our time. The books challenge the assumptions that lie behind the headlines and offer proposals, not always the expected ones, for action.

Already available:
Aids and the Good Society
Patricia Illingworth

Understanding War

W. B. Gallie

London and New York

First published 1991
by Routledge
11 New Fetter Lane, London EC4P 4EE

Simultaneously published in the USA and Canada
by Routledge
a division of Routledge, Chapman and Hall, Inc.
29 West 35th Street, New York, NY 10001

Set in 10/12 Souvenir Light, Linotron 202
Disc conversion by Columns
Printed in England by T. J. Press (Padstow), Cornwall

British Library Cataloguing in Publication Data
Gallie, W.B. (Walter Bryce)
  Understanding war. – (Points of conflict).
  1. War – Sociological perspectives
  I. Title   II. Series
  303.66

Library of Congress Cataloging in Publication Data
Gallie, W. B
  Understanding war / W. B. Gallie.
    p.   cm. — (Points of conflict)
  Includes index.
  1. War. 2. Nuclear warfare. 3. Peace. I. Title. II. Series.
U21.2.G34   1991
303.6′6—dc20   90-8757

  ISBN 0–415–05639–X
  ISBN 0–415–05640–3 pbk

Contents

1 Man as a war-making animal

The title of this chapter echoes a number of famous dicta. Not only the classic 'Man is a rational animal' and 'Man is a political animal', but more recent characterizations of man as 'a religious animal' (Burke), 'a tool-making animal' (Franklin), a 'huckstering animal' (Adam Smith), 'a productive animal' (Marx) and 'a historical animal', in the sense that to be human involves having some kind of history – a claim whose most forceful exponent to date has been R.G. Collingwood.

None of the great men just quoted tried to establish exactly what consequences flowed from his preferred characterization of man. Their concerns were too urgent, as well as somewhat blurred at the edges. Each believed that he had hit upon one aspect of human life whose importance earlier thinkers had neglected, and an examination of which would enable men to see better what improvements they could effect in the world and what assets they could secure in it. It was in this confident spirit that Burke, Franklin, Marx and others laid the foundation of those ideologies whose conflicting claims were later to set so many teeth on edge. They began by opening men's eyes to a number of important continuities and parallels between hitherto seemingly disconnected strands of human endeavour; but they overstretched themselves, and in claiming to tell us everything of importance about man, they gave rise to creeds which are either brutally constricting or feebly platitudinous. Now if this is the case with the famous characterizations of man

1

which I have mentioned, why should we bother with so exotic and cynical a claim as that man is, if only primarily or predominantly, a war-making animal?

From a theoretical standpoint this suggestion may indeed have little to recommend it. It would be implausible to urge that the practice of war explained or underlay or gave birth to or justified all or even most other major human achievements. But from the standpoint of practice, things look rather different. Man's war-making propensity may well deserve our most careful attention, not as a lesson but as a warning. It is hardly necessary to elaborate this point in detail. We all live today, if not under the threat then at least with the ever-present possibility of a war which would turn into a nuclear war, capable of destroying our civilization and perhaps all higher forms of life on the planet. If men should in fact destroy their civilization and habitat as a result of their war-making propensity, then, in an existential sense, that propensity would have proved itself predominant among other human attributes. However brutish and barren of any positive results it may have been, it would have been proved to possess one power – that of total termination – over the rest of human life. The 'bomb' – or other more sophisticated means of nuclear destruction – which would put an end to human life, would *eo ipso* settle the problem, which of mankind's various capacities was most crucial to its story.

To this of course it could be retorted that such a disaster could result from other causes: from some cosmic development quite beyond our power to avoid or control, or some unwitting spoliation of our environment, or some daring experiment – say with a view to energy production – which went tragically wrong. In all these cases, however, the destruction of human life and achievement would be an accident, leaving its inherent values untarnished. But that mankind should destroy itself in the ultimate expression of something of its own devising – the practice of war – suggests an underlying farcicality in the whole human adventure, a farcicality as sickening as it is shaming. Only human groups that have been educated, trained and equipped to destroy each other's warring capacity at *almost any cost* could have landed themselves in the crazy anomaly of our age: namely that men's immensely enlarged control over the forces of Nature should have threatened them within a few decades with their own self-destruction.

Reflection along these lines became commonplace during the years of so-called Cold War. But now, it may be felt, they are mercifully out of season. The nuclear threat which has darkened our minds for over forty years has been notably diminished if not entirely removed. Other anxieties and problems, less urgently menacing but hardly less important, occupy the political foreground and open up new political horizons. When the nations of the world are preoccupied with their economic needs and possibilities and are pressing for their elementary rights, it seems unthinkable that they should be drawn back into destroying each other – and themselves – with nuclear weapons. Yet it takes only a few moments' serious reflection to recognize how naively wishful this way of thinking is. There have been other times – after 1815, and more particularly between 1871 and 1914 – when many European politicians and publicists were talking in something very like this vein. But, as we all know, their commendable hopes did not mean that the motives and occasions of war had vanished from the world. During the last few years we have seen a remarkable abatement in the military rivalry of the super-powers, particularly with respect to nuclear weapons. But again, this movement towards sanity on their part has not brought the danger of nuclear war to an end. War, throughout its history, has shown a capacity to break out anew in unexpected places from unforeseen causes, and often at new levels of destructiveness. The nightmare of the two super-powers blasting each other – and the rest of us – into extinction may have been lifted; but the possibility that they might be dragged by misadventure, misunderstanding and failure of nerve into a nuclear exchange which neither of them wanted, remains to be considered. Besides, there are the three other acknowledged or self-proclaimed nuclear powers, and, perhaps more significant, at least five other rapidly developing industrial powers with barely concealed capacities and plans for future nuclear armament. And there are international terrorist groups which, we may be sure, would greedily accept any bits and pieces of nuclear know-how which might come their way.

During the years of the Cold War these dangers were continually, if ineffectively, being debated. But the inconclusiveness of the so-called nuclear debate – in which each of the three main contestant parties always claimed to be winning, and today claims to have *won!* – makes many of us disinclined to return to such seemingly vain disputation. Hence the danger that the present fortunate lull in the rivalry of the super-powers will be wasted, as we relax in the assumption that the nuclear peril has been passed, or perhaps was never as grave as we imagined it to be. The arguments of this book are directed against this danger. They are designed to show that the problems of the nuclear age are far more deep-rooted, and far more confusingly rooted, in basic human beliefs, practices and institutions, than we like to acknowledge. Two relatively simple observations have recently confirmed this belief in me. First, very few discussions of the nuclear problem have even tried to relate its paradoxes and uncertainties to those of earlier 'classic wars'. In other words the nuclear problem is usually considered out of its historical context, and without reference to certain inherent features of war which have persisted through all its astonishing changes. But secondly, the number of books that seriously engage with the 'concept of war', puzzling over its apparent contradictions and struggling to achieve a synoptic view of its many-sided developments, can be counted on one hand and (I am inclined sometimes to think) on one or two fingers of one hand. Why should this be so?

War, to a superficial analysis, is such an elementary, familiar and seemingly irremovable thing, neither requiring nor provoking reflective thought. Like sex for our Victorian forebears, war is something so obviously important and yet so terrifying that conventional wisdom suggests that the less it is thought about the better. The result is that war, even today, is less a topic of human thought than an area of human non-thinking, in spite of the countless books about it that pour out from the press. Men have, of course, romanticized war, and have revelled imaginatively in its dramatic twists and turns, climaxes and reversals, and on many minds the gadgetry of war in any age exercises a powerful fascination. But this does not amount to thinking about war seriously – about what it is, about why it has persisted through so many extraordinary changes and developments and about why it has to date resisted or evaded almost all efforts to control and contain it. Again, while there have of course been serious histories of wars, these have been written, for the most part, from the particular standpoint of the nations concerned – their needs, their ambitions or their very survival. For this reason most histories of war fail to notice the larger pattern of change – in the overall character and potentiality of war – within which their special topics and problems have arisen. Their interest, they could quite properly claim, is in wars not War. Indeed it is only since war has come to be seen as a threat to life on this planet, that its identity and the basic springs of its growth have become matters of vital concern to mankind.

It is not easy, however, to persuade people that they have not begun to think seriously or to any real purpose about one of their own most notable practices; the more so after they have been subjected to years of strenuous and seemingly endless debate over how the menace of nuclear war might be contained or lessened or perhaps finally removed. This is why, in the chapter that follows, I continue with that at present flagging but by no means finished nuclear debate; but not with a view to providing any of the three main parties to it with a new and convincing proof of its own rightness. On the contrary, my exposition of their respective cases, although not unsympathetic, is intended to show that the debate has continued because none of them is logically acceptable and that each derives its vitality chiefly from its passionate – and up to a point proper – rejection of the other two. This situation is due, on the logical side, to the one thing which the three main parties to the debate have in common: a quite uncritical belief that the nuclear problem is essentially simple and single and admits of only one kind of approach and treatment – political (say those who see little hope of extensive nuclear disarmament), moral (say the unilateral nuclear disarmers), technical or strategic (say those analysts who concentrate their thought on the peculiar 'genius' of nuclear weapons). It is for this reason – because the nuclear problem is placed in different fundamental compartments or categories of human thinking – that the arguments of the main parties to the debate flash past each other, with no apparent communicative or persuasive effects, like express trains on parallel rail-tracks. On the psychological side, the belief that rescue from this nuclear peril must lie in a single means or route is much more easily explained. When men are faced with a sudden, seemingly unprecedented danger, their natural reaction is to look for some single simple cause of it and defence against it, and any deviation from their own chosen method of meeting it seems to them to be foolishness or half-heartedness or even betrayal. Now, add to this the fact, already mentioned, that there is no established tradition of critical thinking about war's ever-changing character, and it is not difficult to see why the nuclear debate has been so unproductive of real results, and, for this reason, why the present lull in the rivalry of the super-powers and their arms-race may be so misleading.

But even if this line of argument (which I develop more fully in chapter 2) is accepted, it nevertheless leaves open the possibility that one of the above approaches to the nuclear problem – say the political approach – is the *correct* one, even though it is (tragically) impossible for the other parties in this debate to see that this is so. But, as I shall show, this possibility is ruled out by the fact that none of the approaches just mentioned is capable of getting at the heart – or the throat – of the nuclear problem, and this is because none of them comprises or rests upon an adequate idea of how nuclear weapons have arisen from, and indeed have given final expression to, the inherent tendency of war – considered as a continuous dimension of human practice – to escalate towards ever more total, that is final, levels of violence. This process, which I discuss in the central chapter of this book, seems to me to be one of the great neglected themes in the history of mankind. It has been possible to neglect it chiefly because war has hitherto been essentially a local and sporadically recurrent affair. But now that the use of nuclear weapons threatens the survival of mankind, it is no longer possible to think of war simply as a recurrent scourge, shadowing and chilling the sunnier phases of human life. The wrongs and horrors of past wars may have long cried out against war's continuance, but they will cry out in vain unless we succeed in articulating to ourselves, with a new fullness and clarity, the ever elusive, because ever changing, character of war, and its place in human affairs. Hence the main line of argument of this book. In chapter 3 I offer an overall sketch of the ways in which war has come to figure in mankind's self-image as one of the great inescapables of human life, about which we can do virtually nothing; and in chapter 4 I try to show how, side by side with certain initially irresistible services and attractions, war quickly displayed those features which pointed in the direction of its ever-increasing destructiveness. However much other human advances, notably in technology and political organization, have contributed to this process, its central drive, I shall argue, is inherent in the operation of war itself. And in chapter 5 I examine the stultifying effects of this process upon both the practice and the theory of international politics.

On the basis of these arguments I put forward in my two concluding chapters some constructive ideas about how war, and in particular nuclear war, can be brought under rational control. In so far as my ideas on this score are political, their purpose is, of course, not to present what should be done – this must always wait upon opportunity – but to indicate certain kinds or directions of action which are generally ignored. In politics there are always more alternatives than politicians are aware of – until the terrible day when someone upsets the apple-cart and shows the appalling inadequacy of their assumptions and concerns.

In so far as my ideas are educational, I can speak more directly. I find it an absurd anomaly that, at the end of a century shaken by two world wars, War Studies should be pursued only on a narrowly specialist basis, while Peace Studies, with two or three honourable exceptions, have no place in most British universities and polytechnics. My suggestion that these two branches of study should be brought closer together and made available to all students engaged in higher education, will of course be greeted with scorn in many academic quarters. But scorn in these quarters is all too often a cloak for fear of change: and the changes which I am advocating are no mere gimmicks aimed at quick political and financial returns. They are put forward as a new form of the unending battle against 'sleep and damnation' (the sleep of the damned being, in this nuclear age, the sleep from which nobody will awake).

However my arguments may be received, I am quite confident about their starting-point. Our situation, vis-à-vis war today, is unparalleled in two closely related respects. The first is obvious. Nuclear war is capable of bringing the whole human adventure to nothing, and the task of preventing this has an urgency which, for the foreseeable future, amounts to paramountcy. But secondly, this task cannot be usefully approached without a constant appreciation of what war has made of man, and of the depth and tenacity of its hold upon so many areas of human life. Man the war-making animal, the inventor but by no means the controller of war as an instrument of politics, can survive war in its most developed forms only by mastering it in thought before it drags him down in self-destruction. And if this should turn out to be as arduous and wearisome a task as manual labour and social compliance have been in the past, so be it. Men can survive only as long as they do not forget what they have found themselves to be capable of doing. Perhaps, indeed, man is the kind of animal that, for all his capacity for imagination and invention, can find his true status only in coping with an enemy which he feels to be his *last* enemy. Today that enemy is not individual death, nor yet the death of any particular group or faith or nation. It is the death of the whole human enterprise, through an unforgivable fecklessness towards the priceless gift of human life.

2 The underlying fallacy in the nuclear debate

The phrase 'the nuclear debate' suggests that there is a relatively clear and distinct nuclear problem admitting of a rationally acceptable solution. But in fact the invention and deployment of nuclear weapons has presented mankind with a whole new problematic area in which some of the most important compartments or categories of our thinking – political, moral, technical and strategic – seem to have been crushed and telescoped together in ways that make lucid thinking extremely difficult. The result is that we find complete oppositions of opinion as to where the nuclear problem should be placed within these familiar great divisions of human concern. Thus, during recent decades, we have heard authoritative voices pronouncing – chiefly against overweening moralists and strategists – that the nuclear rivalry between west and east is primarily a political matter and can be resolved only by a satisfactory political settlement. But, of course, we have heard equally authoritative-sounding pronouncements from the moralists, to the effect that the issue is, on the contrary, primarily a moral one, since in no conceivable circumstances can the use of nuclear weapons be morally sanctioned. And we have also heard from the strategists that it is only by appreciating the peculiar genius of the new weapons, and the limits of their effective use, that we can find an escape-route from our nuclear nightmares.

I want now to show not only that each of these claims is

11

suspect because it ignores the prima-facie force and at least partial relevance of the others; but that each, however worthy its ancestry, manifestly fails to stand up in, and to be equal to the needs of, the nuclear age. Each gains what plausibility it possesses by ignoring facts and implications of facts which no one can deny but which no one knows how to combine in a single synoptic vision or model of the current human situation.

The political claim

To begin, then, with the claim that the nuclear problem is primarily political. For at least two hundred years the practice of international politics has been subject to two radically opposed interpretations: the idealist or legalistic on the one hand, the power-political on the other. The former is based, to speak very roughly, on liberal principles derived from domestic politics. Its aim has been to infuse some degree of order, security and justice, by means of negotiation, binding treaties and the acceptance of mediation and arbitration into the traditional turmoil of international rivalry and war. More particularly it has pinned its faith on progressive balanced disarmament between the strongest military powers. The second interpretation claims to condense the simple if painful lessons of international history. These are that, while in all serious international conflicts the will of the stronger prevails, usually by means of war, war is notoriously a risky and costly business, so that skill in international politics consists in confining it to the most serious conflicts of interests. This can be done by ensuring that, in any given area and period, there is no doubt about where predominant power lies and in what circumstances it will be used. In other words, it is always up to the strongest power to make its weight felt – not necessarily, however, by throwing it around in a vulgarly ostentatious fashion. Cromwell, Frederick II and Bismarck are commonly cited as masters of power politics in the international field.

Both these interpretations of international politics have civilized aims and have at times been of service to mankind. But both were patently brain-children of the pre-nuclear world in which the occurrence of wars between the greatest military powers, although usually a disaster, was nevertheless something which there was no direct and watertight method of precluding. The possibility of occasional great wars entered, explicitly and indeed by definition, into the world-view of power-politics: the impossibility of guaranteeing peace in all circumstances, even after the general acceptance of the best international procedures, meant that war had to be countenanced as a last resort by even the most confident international legalists and idealists. Both these positions were, in the light of past international practice, entirely intelligible. But neither stands up in a world which can be destroyed in a matter of weeks if not days as a result of nuclear war. The power-political interpretation lost its credibility, for sane and sensitive minds, as a result of World War I, while the hopes of international idealists were badly dented by the failures of the League of Nations in the inter-war years.

In point of fact, neither interpretation has been wholeheart-edly embraced by any major power since 1945. In particular, the super-powers have oscillated, unhappily, and with a poor grace, between them. When things are going smoothly they at least pay lip-service to idealist/legalist principles, but they return quickly to power-politics as soon as real difficulties arise. The result is that international politics have latterly become a fudge of two approaches, neither of which was designed for or is capable of coping with the peculiar dangers of the nuclear age. Perhaps this fudge was inevitable, in view of the terrors and uncertainties which have faced statesmen of west and east since 1945; but it has led to an unfortunately widespread cynicism about the possibility of improving international relations. International politics, to the popular mind, are a stage on which statesmen meet and make flowery speeches, while backstage – or above or below stage – preparations are being made to blow the whole show to smithereens. For my present purpose, however, which is to demonstrate the inadequacy of currently accepted political approaches to the nuclear problem, it is best to treat the two interpretations (or versions) of international politics separately.

To begin, this time, with the power-political approach. As soon as Russia obtained nuclear weapons it was evident that power-politics must now be played with a difference. Superior power could no longer be demonstrated by a readiness to use force – in the form of nuclear weapons – since this would be suicidal for both parties. What either party could do, however, was to show that it would never allow itself to be *dis*advantaged as a world-power by its inability to respond to, if not to equal, its rival's nuclear strength. And, of course, this shared determination led, as inevitably if less directly than open preparation for nuclear war would have done, to the nuclear arms-race, in which either party believed that it could crack its rival's morale – in economic if not in military terms – so that it would one day cry 'Hold, enough!' (The thought that this might happen almost simultaneously to both parties, appears not to have occurred to anyone until the first of the Gorbachev–Reagan summits took place.) It is easy, however, as we look over the years of the Cold War and after, to see that this variant of power-politics to match the nuclear age, was fatally flawed from the outset. First, it ignored the fact that, while a political victory and enduring settlement were its ultimate aims, the prolonged struggle and sacrifice by which those aims were to be achieved, must progressively deepen and sharpen the rivalry of the two contestants. Hence, at every stage on the road to that intended settlement the likelihood of a fatal nuclear outbreak – through miscalculation or misreading or through sheer failure of nerve or animal desperation – is likely to be increasing. If ever there was a case of an end not justifying its means, it was here. Equally, it assumed that while a trial-by-arms-race proceeds, no other new factors can arise to confuse and even transform the situation. In particular it ignored the possible effects of a proliferation of nuclear weapons – even if outmoded and of doubtful efficiency – to other nations or groups of nations whose interests and ambitions the super-powers have arrogantly ignored. Smaller nations cannot of course hope to rival the super-powers in the number and accuracy of their nuclear weapons; but this does not mean that they cannot adapt nuclear technology to their own local purposes with globally disastrous effects. Finally, what of the moral effect – the effect on human *morale* – of the sight of the world's two greatest powers straining their resources to the limit and risking the future of mankind in a race for supremacy, whose results are impossible to foresee? For this reason, it seems to me, the attempt to update traditional power-politics to meet the dangers of the nuclear age, was radically misconceived. The political methods of a Frederick II or a Bismarck, remarkable in their own ways in their own days, can contribute nothing to the solution of problems which, even when they appear to be local and transient, are potentially global and terminal.

Can anything better be expected, then, from the rival interpretation of international problems which claims that they are resolvable by negotiations aimed at securing the essential interests of the parties concerned? This interpretation, it must be admitted, seems to gain support from the one unquestioned achievement of the modern world: the creation of a world economic order based on a network of treaties between independent states, supported by a number of original international institutions, and displaying a remarkable degree of reliability, legality and even, on certain issues, an inspired humanity. But on the matter of war between nations, and of the ever increasing destructiveness of war when waged and supported by the most powerful nations, it too has proved bitterly disappointing. War, liberal international idealists have believed, could be limited and in the end eliminated by a process of ordered mutual disarmament between the world's leading powers. Stripped of their weapons, nations would find better methods of patching up their quarrels. What a cruel comment on this hope has been provided by our classic century of war! What, then, was wrong with it? And what remains wrong with even the most recent efforts to revive it?

This hoped-for end was bound to fail for five distinct although inter-related reasons. I begin with the most currently pertinent of these. Given a deep-seated rivalry between two nations or blocs of nations, each will always be tempted to deceive the other – and perhaps itself – by advertising its reductions of weapon-systems which are already outmoded, while improving and in effect transforming other weapon-systems which, it believes, will dominate the future. Equally important, in this technological age, is the fear that some altogether new military development will become available to one side or the other which will suddenly alter the assumptions and the trust upon which all progress in disarmament depends. And this points to the objection which has been so often effectively raised against unilateral nuclear disarmers, but which applies only a little less obviously to all policies which see in nuclear disarmament the only escape from nuclear war. No invention can be un-invented; hence no weapon-system which two or more nations have agreed to discard is ever finally eliminated. It, or some hideously 'improved' version of it, can always be brought back into action. Moreover, a scramble to be first in reassembling any such system could well prove more dangerous, in the way of creating panic distrust, than an uninterrupted development of it would have been. And, to move to a more general level of argument, even if a programme of balanced nuclear disarmament between the super-powers were to be worked out successfully, would it do anything more than bring the parties involved back to the situation which obtained before their last bout of competitive rearmament began? For instance, supposing that the super-powers should succeed during the next decade in reducing their nuclear armaments to zero, would this mean an end of their political rivalry? As with very powerful individuals, so with very powerful nations: it takes unusually strong bonds to bring them into, and to keep them in, amity. Which points to what is perhaps the deepest objection of all. Is not the idea of progressive, and even of total nuclear disarmament lacking in positively cohesive power? What it urges, although important, is something altogether negative: a removal, a diminution, a withdrawal. It contains no hint or spark of creative promise. And one is left wondering: can any immense obstacle or danger be overcome without the vision of something positively rewarding to replace it?

If now we consider together the objections to both these traditional interpretations of international politics, what stands out as their most important common weakness? I have already remarked that both are evidently products of the pre-nuclear world. Their uncertainties and loop-holes could be tolerated so long as war – even on a Napoleonic scale – was itself still tolerable. But after the two total wars of our century and in the midst of our nuclear anxieties their familiar maxims and nostrums sound worse than hollow, their ineffectuality is almost insulting. Wars that tear apart and are capable of terminating life on this planet are a different story from even the most fiendishly cruel (but fortunately local) wars of earlier ages. And as the scale and destructiveness of war have changed its political connotation, so have men's moral responses to it. The command 'Thou shalt not kill' has a different level or depth of meaning when applied today to the extermination of whole non-combatant populations, from that which it bore when applied to the bloodiest battle-fields of the past. The significance of this change has not been lost to the bulk of mankind, hesitant and timid though the acceptance of it may be. The idea of survival is no longer limited to kith and kin or to one particular area of the world's surface; it is common knowledge that the new weapons are indifferent to frontiers and fortifications; and there is a growing sense that problems of defence and security have now been stretched to cover humanity as a whole. Yet the traditionally acknowledged and available principles, moves and methods of international politics take no account of these changes. For political realists, they are so much chaff which will be scattered at the first report or threat of war. And for international idealists, the only possible restrictions on war are treaties between states which retain their separate forces for their separate purposes, should negotiation or arbitration prove unavailing. What is patently lacking in both approaches is any idea of how the new weapons – or the technology which supports them – can be harnessed to ensure what the waking moral perception of mankind demands: namely that these weapons shall never again be used for the traditional ends of war.

The moral claim

The claim that the nuclear problem is primarily a moral one has an attractive simplicity which is enhanced by the humane earnestness of those who propound it. Yet they have failed significantly to carry more than a small minority in Britain and most other countries to a complete acceptance of their views. And this, I shall argue, is not due simply to the moral inertia, cowardice, stupidity or plain perversity of those whom they impress but do not convince. Painful though it is to criticize those to whom so much credit is due, it is of the first importance to see where and why the claims of most 'unilateral nuclear disarmers' break down. As I shall try to show, the simplicity and earnestness of their position has something dangerously constricting and misleading about it.

Nuclear weapons are usually justified by those who possess them on the ground that the *threat* of using them is the only way of preventing their *actual* use. Yet threats work only if they are seriously intended: which is why every nuclear power does what it can to make its enemies believe that in certain circumstances it would use its nuclear weapons against them. One of the effects of this policy, however, is to intensify the hostility and distrust which gave rise to the original nuclear rivalry. Not only is it, thus far, a self-contradictory policy, it is one which, as it is pursued, induces a kind of self-deception from which it is very difficult to escape. Indeed a government which proclaims – even if not in so many words – that there are no lengths in indiscriminate and perhaps irreversible destructiveness to which it would not go for the sake of preserving its own most cherished values, is not far from the edge of moral insanity. It is not far from the position of the man who, claiming to love his fellows but rightly believing that power corrupts, feels that he must therefore reduce them all to the condition of slaves. When thus expounded, the nuclear problem does seem to be primarily a moral problem: namely that of getting the great majority of mankind, first in one's own country and ultimately throughout the world, to recognize nuclear weapons for what they are – the instruments of incomparable evil. Only when this is done, will it be worthwhile engaging in questions about how to dismantle and dispose of them, how to alter national policies and to secure rights and interests which nuclear weapons have been thought to defend, and to persuade recalcitrant governments into making these changes.

There is so much that is of value in this claim, which has been developed, both in religious and in lay terms, by powerful thinkers in many western countries, that to criticize it seems almost perverse. Yet criticize it we must since it displays, quite as much as do any other one-sided claims, the inchoation or lack of all-round preparation in our thinking about war which this book seeks to criticize and correct. In treating the nuclear problem primarily – and often purely – as a moral problem, and in regarding all political and strategic aspects of it as so many distractions, it *eo ipso* allies itself to another attitude of mind, radically opposed to both the political and strategic, yet quite as liable as they are to mislead and to betray.

This attitude is commonly called Apocalyptic. It sees the

immediate danger of nuclear war and destruction as the climax of the long history of war, and as the ultimate proof of the evil in the world. The first demand of moral sanity is that nuclear weapons shall be denounced, then renounced, unconditionally. Until that is done any apparent step forward will be a kind of backsliding.

Apocalyptic denunciations are patently not scientific predictions. They are not based on a general theory which can be tested and reformulated as the evidence requires. They always warn of some particular and catastrophic change. An all-dominating empire will perish without a trace. An authoritarian system of religion will crumble before claims of individual conscience. Capitalism will collapse under the weight of its own successes. And, similarly, mastery of nuclear energy will destroy the scientific civilization which evolved it. These claims are not to be compared with experimental science. Each of them springs from an impassioned hypnotic vision of human society, having as its focus a catastrophe which, although imprecisely dated, is promised for the very near future. They have a now-or-never quality, and they dictate not so much what must be done as that something quite unparalleled must be done, and be done quickly.

Of course, many Apocalyptic prophecies have turned out to be false, and in retrospect seem childish. The world did not come to an end during the first century AD, or after the first millennium. On the other hand we should remember how many mighty institutions have collapsed with appalling suddenness and for reasons which might well have made them prime targets for Apocalyptic denunciation. And to this we must add that today's warnings of a nuclear catastrophe are at least consistent with a vast array of evidence which makes all talk of exaggeration or fantasy in this regard carry with it a whiff of carelessness that is either criminal or insane.

But now we must notice the kind of morality, or moral outlook, which Apocalyptic prophecy is likely to support. It is not always world-rejecting, but it is always, to a marked degree, a morality which appeals to those for whom the world seems to be at a standstill, or for whom all society's serious concerns are already wrapped up and covered in the vision of an impending and deserved disaster. Such an outlook has the effect of convincing its adherents that there is nothing more that they need to find out about the conditions or progress of the coming calamity, nothing more that they must try out or learn to do, or to do better, during the 'run-up' period between the promulgation of the prophecy and its expected realization. The great calamity will bring an end to history as men have known it, therefore recognition of its imminence shows the pointlessness of all further questioning, as well as of all self-doubt and self-criticism. The spell is wound up: the prophesy is taken to be logically sufficient as a basis for all serious human thought and action.

The dangers involved in this way of thinking are obvious. It refuses to consider questions, the pursuit of which might help us to resist, contain or divert the threatened catastrophe. Apocalyptic prophecies suggest that everything has been said that needs to be said once the likelihood of the future nuclear disaster has been made plain. They thus inculcate a belief-pattern which shies away from ideas, arguments and projects which might in any way distract attention from their central claim. In fine, too much moralistic thinking about nuclear weapons is focused upon *that* day when the Apocalyptic prophecy will be vindicated, rather than on *this* day when the disaster, which so properly obsesses so many good people, can still, perhaps, be forestalled. The primarily moral approach to the nuclear problem has produced timely warnings of the appalling range of irresponsible action that has been opened up by the invention of nuclear weapons. But by conceiving the nuclear problem too narrowly, its advocates run the risk of falling into the irresponsibility of believing that there is nothing more to be learnt about the problem, and nothing more to be done about it than they themselves are doing. This is the irresponsibility of fanaticism – and of the *unco guid*.

The technical and strategic claim

The claim that the nuclear problem is primarily strategic, since it is caused by the peculiar genius of nuclear weapons, is logically simpler than either of the two claims so far considered. Nevertheless it demands more careful preliminary clarification than they did. Nobody suggests that it is nuclear weapons themselves which by their simple existence threaten humanity. Everyone agrees that it is the men behind the weapons, or the men behind the men with the weapons, who cause the trouble. Nevertheless, it seems perfectly legitimate, in order to highlight the peculiar features of nuclear war, to make the greatest possible abstraction from the social and political factors involved, and to concentrate attention on the features of nuclear weapons which render them so indiscriminately destructive, so disturbing of past political assumptions, as well as morally intolerable. Thus, in the approach now to be considered, a deliberate effort is made to reduce those who direct and man nuclear forces to the level of mere operatives − by hand or brain − of the strategies which nuclear weapons have (allegedly) imposed upon the governments and peoples of the most powerful nations of the world. This is, in effect, to claim that human beings − or at least the citizens of the most industrially developed sections of mankind − are more or less the slaves of the new weapons which they have created. And this claim, if taken seriously, would seem to rest on the wider assumption, that the history of mankind has always been directed, as well as limited, by the technologies available to men. But without involving ourselves at this stage in these extreme views, we can readily admit that the kind of abstraction − or, in the mathematical sense, the kind of 'idealization' − which we here encounter, may well be necessary as a first step if we are to understand the peculiar, and in many respects paradoxical, situation which today faces mankind.

What, then, are the peculiar features of nuclear weapons?

One was obvious from the start, one was quickly recognized by clear-sighted analysts, a third, more ambiguous and delusive, gave rise to the hope that nuclear weapons, for all the horror which they inspired, had in fact made full-scale – global, total – war impossible ever after.

Obvious from the start was the incomparable destructive power of the new weapons, against which no defence, in the traditional sense, seemed possible. To be sure, other great military innovations had given rise to similar fears – the horse, the war-chariot, mobile artillery, for example. But in this instance, the magnitude of the new destructive power was of a different order from that of all its predecessors. Earlier military innovations had rendered their victims helpless and horror-struck, but the range of their destructiveness had been limited and short-lived, and they quickly became part of the standard equipment of warfare. By contrast, nuclear weapons threaten destruction which is at once instant and irreversible, accurately pinpointed and yet global in its effects.

In place of traditional means of defence against nuclear weapons there was, however, another possibility: retaliation in kind. The threat of this, it was argued, could provide a complete check to the use of nuclear weapons. And thus was born the doctrine of nuclear deterrence, upon which, although with notable differences in its possible means of operation, all nuclear powers have relied for the last thirty odd years. The only counter to nuclear threats or blackmail, it was generally agreed, was the possession of a nuclear force at least comparable to that of any possible assailant. Unfortunately, this counter to nuclear threats is itself faced with a formidable objection. In a technologically fertile age nuclear rivals will inevitably compete by improving their weapons in both quality and quantity. Hence the old adage 'If you want peace, prepare for war' becomes in the nuclear age 'If you want peace, you must prepare yourself for even bigger, costlier wars.' More simply, you are committed to a nuclear arms-race; and no government to date has succeeded in seeing its way round this difficulty, even though they are appalled by the prospect that it opens up. The result is that the kind of peace that is supported by nuclear counter-threats has proved to be as costly as it is unnerving.

From this impasse one intellectually attractive escape-route was explored by a number of strategic analysts during the 1950s and early 60s. This aimed at giving a new conclusiveness and bite to the hopeful but vague thesis that nuclear weapons have only one sane purpose: to ensure that they are never in fact unleashed in war. The problem was, how could two deterrent nuclear forces discharge this function without involving their possessors in a continuous arms-race. An ingenious answer was found in the idea of a limit beyond which further development of either nuclear force would be, not so much immoral or politically disastrous, as strategically pointless and absurd. For (so it was postulated) beyond that point each side, even if subjected to a devastating surprise attack, would retain a sufficient 'unviolated' nuclear force to return an equally devastating blow at its aggressor. What had suggested this idea was, of course, less the number or power of the actual nuclear weapons available than the mobility and untrackable nature of their delivery systems. But, irrespective of the particular form which the doctrine of Mutually Assured Destructive Capability (MADC) took on, its originality lay in its claim that the peculiar genius of the new weapons itself pointed the way out of the nightmare of nuclear terror. As with many other bold advances in thought, the doctrine of MADC advanced in the right direction, but with no adequate awareness of its many-sided implications. What was sound in it was the recognition that nuclear weapons, being of a different order of destructiveness from any previously devised by men, must inevitably affect our received conception of war. War had previously been regarded as a logically simple, although many-purpose, instrument whose *modus operandi* was to achieve superiority through victory in battle. But in the kind of situation which was postulated by MADC such superiority was unachievable.

Neither side in an all-out nuclear exchange could render its opponents any 'deader' than it would be itself. The key question therefore had become this: could the limiting point at which further nuclear strength became pointless for either of two rival powers be clearly defined and securely maintained? And the main weakness of the doctrine of MADC was to assume that this limiting-point could be defined on a clear if not altogether simple numerical basis. Moreover advocates of the doctrine seem to have believed that once the limiting-point was reached, either side, being now invulnerable, could rely on a policy of 'pure' deterrence: i.e. 'pure' in the sense that its nuclear forces, like its heart and hands, could be free of all suspicion of aggressive intent. Either power (to re-state this point rather simplistically) would be in a position to sit back in almost passive security, thanks to its recognized capacity to react to any aggression with devastating retaliatory power. Thus, the special character of the new weapons, as indicated in the doctrine of MADC, points to the possibility of a stable balance between rival nuclear powers which was unimaginable for as long as each entertained the hope of achieving complete superiority through an escalation of its forces, whether in terms of numbers or in destructive power.

Although probably retained as the rationale of American nuclear policy for a number of years, the doctrine of MADC was never wholeheartedly espoused by either of the super-powers. To politico-military bureaucrats it no doubt seemed too clever to be true; and in any case it contained loop-holes which politico-military horse-sense could smell out even if it could not identify them clearly. Certainly throughout the 1960s and 1970s and early 1980s the nuclear arms-race proceeded apace; and even today, when great efforts are being made to restrain and revise it, it is far from clear what part the doctrine of MADC plays in the calculations of the super-powers. It is therefore of the first importance to distinguish clearly what is of value in the doctrine – what it contributes to the hope of human survival in the nuclear age

– from certain relatively simple oversights which have detracted from its value.

First and most obviously, it ignores the fact that every deterrent weapon or weapon-system is liable to be eroded with time. Not only have weapons to be replaced, but replacement in an age of frantic technological progress usually means improvement in accuracy and destructive power, which become steadily more important than sheer numerical expansion. Thus the military establishments of rival powers, even when instructed by their governments to maintain a strict balance of nuclear weapons, are liable to keep the treadmill of rearmament in motion. Here are grounds for the kind of political suspicion and friction which the doctrine of MADC claimed to eliminate from the nuclear problem. And this difficulty at once points to others, less clear-cut but not less dangerous. Calculations of a military balance, whether in weaponry or in man-power, have always to take into account factors of a not obviously or directly military kind: in particular changes in the diplomatic, demographic, industrial and technological advantages enjoyed by the parties concerned. An agreement between two nuclear powers, based on the doctrine of MADC, might perhaps manage to take account of all such complicating factors. But it is impossible to imagine this happening without a positive *will-to-agreement* between the parties, which in turn requires some degree of sympathy and trust between them. Indeed, I think that one can go further than this and claim that without a *will-to-co-operate positively*, in a joint policy for nuclear security, the kind of passive balance between two nuclear powers which the doctrine of MADC envisages simply could not be maintained. The proponents of MADC have been right to insist that the special character and capacities of nuclear weapons have made an agreed balance something more than an abstract possibility – something at once more morally urgent and more politically practicable than could previously have been foreseen. This new situation, however, remains something that has to be exploited constructively if nuclear rivalry and distrust are to be overcome. The dangers of nuclear weaponry have begun to awaken popular thinking in many countries to new moral responsibilities, but they have hardly stirred the minds of governments to the need of new political initiatives, devices and institutions to implement and secure worldwide nuclear peace. What form these initiatives and institutions should take, I shall be discussing in chapter 6.

The upshot is, therefore, that as much as with the primarily political and the primarily moral approaches to the nuclear problem, the primarily strategic or military approach is unacceptable, not simply because of its manifest loop-holes but because it fails to match up to the all-roundness and Protean complexity of the problem. Indeed, even more than with the two previous approaches, the proposed solution based on the idea of MADC shows the dangers of intellectual compartmentalizations when we are dealing with the topic of war. For not only is war, in Clausewitz's phrase, a veritable chameleon, changing its outward shape with every change in its background. The main direction of all its major changes – towards ever greater destructiveness – demands corresponding change in the political, moral and economic thought-habits which motivate it, support it and seek to control it. Hence the need, which I shall try to meet in the chapters that now follow, for a more synoptic vision of the development of war – both in its physical reality and in men's mental reactions to it – than the one which we usually carry about with us. Or, to restate the argument of this chapter more combatively, there is no primarily political, no primarily moral, no primarily strategic answer to the nuclear problem. This is because the invention and deployment of nuclear weapons have revealed in much starker forms than our forefathers could have suspected certain fatal flaws in the political and moral and strategic doctrines by which to date they have tried to limit if not to justify the horrendous dangers of war. Their political endeavours – and ours – have failed to take into account the potentially cumulative and hence self-destructive character of war; their moral criticisms of war neglect the hard truth that there are certain abuses of force which can be forestalled only by skilfully contrived counter-force; and the acutest strategic insights neglect the factors of trust and co-operative enthusiasm without which no great human enterprise can be carried through. What these failings suggest is that war, as it has grown and continues to grow, mocks at all our political, moral and strategic attempts to control it; and that it will continue to do so until we have a much firmer and clearer grasp of war's place − its potentially ever-expanding place − in human affairs. If we are to subjugate and control the mocking monster, we have first to understand it: to have a much more adequate picture of how and why men have created it and what it has made of men. Hence the need for the overall survey of war and of our received idea of it, which I attempt in the chapter which follows.

③ Our received idea of war

The temptation to speculate about war's origins may be irresistible, but its results are disappointing. There is virtually no evidence and the very meaning of the quest is ambiguous. For both these reasons our intuitions – our sense of what might have happened slipping into a conviction of what must have happened – are here quite untrustworthy. Nevertheless such speculation raises a number of points which are worth keeping in mind.

In the first place, the pre-history of mankind must have been, in contrast to its recorded history, a largely non-military one. A history of what we call war might, if only we had the evidence, take us back some six thousand years. But a general history of mankind would cover a vastly larger time-span. So far as can be judged, sheer lack of organization, technology, transport, supplies and surplus population, would have made war unfeasible until the later Neolithic age. No doubt human breeding and feeding groups, like individual humans, have always been prone to aggressiveness, pugnacity and revenge. They may always have been subject (as chimpanzees are said to be) to bouts of group-ferocity and destructiveness, leading to group-massacre. But such outbursts do not mean war as we understand it: viz. organized armed struggle between groups in which each side seeks to displace or dispel, to dominate or to punish, or simply to be rid of the other, by inflicting what we call 'defeat'. War, as we understand it, requires some kind of political purpose, if only of the most rudimentary kind. No doubt, if it had been feasible, earlier human groups would have taken to war, as we know it, as zestfully as their descendants were to do. But fortunately it was not feasible while human populations were small and scattered. Otherwise mankind could easily have destroyed itself before it had developed all the other skills upon which civilization depends.

But to return to the simple question of war's origins. We cannot be certain how the main features of warfare – weapons, strategy, order, training and discipline, political direction and rewards – were brought together into a single art or practice. Nor do we know whether war's characteristic skills were borrowed from the experience of hunting, or from primitive games or rituals. And while it seems likely that human groups acted *as if* (to our ways of thinking) they were at war long before they recognized the special character of what they were doing, it is possible that the idea of war, engaged in for a definite political purpose, came in a flash of genius to some Stone-Age Machiavelli, whereas recognition of what they were in for came only gradually to his slower-witted companions. Again, who knows what was the object of the first sustained and long-remembered war? Was it women – or perhaps one woman? Or children to be saved and used as slaves? Or the need for new territories as population expanded and as former habitats became exhausted – which presumably caused mankind's extraordinary propensity to spread across the globe? Or did war proper begin (as Clausewitz suggested) not from marauding and aggression, but when the 'weak defender' hit on the idea of organized resistance in order to give the aggressor a taste of his own medicine? We do not know and cannot hope to know.

What seems clear, however, is that men are not war-making animals by genetic endowment, but that war is a product of human culture, transmitted and developed over a relatively short span of time. And this implies that over countless millennia men walked the earth, hunted and gathered, crossed the narrow seas, raised their children and dealt with their dead, without recourse to war. Yet to this suggestion of a long primal innocence we must add that in its pre-military stage mankind almost certainly lacked that sense of belonging to an established political order, which is so important to the consciousness of later civilized men. And this begs the question: what brought the pre-military phase of human history to an end?

Again, the details are lost beyond recovery. But there is certainly some truth in Montesquieu's famous dictum: 'Once in a political society, men lose their feeling of weakness: whereupon their former equality disappears and the *state of war* begins.' What makes this dictum at once so astonishing and so persuasive? On the surface it seems to be a boldly simplified account of how the state and war came into existence in a kind of symbiosis. But it also claims to explain the paradox that states provide their subjects with relative security at home only at the cost of almost constant wars with rival states abroad. To expand this point a little: Montesquieu's dictum implies that the burden of continuous government upon any group of people is rendered acceptable by the new sense of corporate strength which it engenders among them. However, this new strength is felt and exercised mainly in face of other competing groups, likewise organized and strengthened through the acceptance of continuous rule. In other words, in becoming political, human beings identify themselves not simply *with* a particular political unit but potentially *against* other competing units: political adhesion turns the subject into a soldier, and the foreigner into a foe.

Yet despite its persuasiveness this answer can be misleading. It presents the state and war as, roughly speaking, two sides of the same coin or as partners in a symbiosis which is permanently and equally necessary to each. But symbiosis on these terms is rare. In human affairs as much as in nature, it is usually confined to certain phases in the life cycle of the forms involved and is also much more evidently indispensable to one form than to another (e.g. to the parasite than to the host). It is easy to see that this is the case with the state and war. The idea of war *logically* requires the idea of the state or continual government – if war is to be distinguished from mere mayhem or brigandage. But the dependence of the state upon war, although unquestionable at many stages in the history of most states, is not of the same logically clear-cut kind. It varies from instance to instance; it is sometimes problematic and it has to be established, not by reference to common usage and belief, but in the light of positive evidence and of careful historical assessment. Thus the upshot is that, even if war and the state arose together, and even if the state has required war to help it establish itself on the human scene, this dependence is not necessarily per-petual. To assume that it must be so is like assuming that because good family relations require that children shall learn habits of obedience, such habits must remain the basis of family happiness when the children have grown up.

This point is of such importance that it is worth re-stating it from a different angle. The existence of firmly established political societies must have been due in some measure to imitation: i.e., different political forms and practices must have competed for favour within a plurality of embryonic states. But such differences, so important for political advancement, were equally important as causes of war: human societies being just as prone to distrust and fear one another as to imitate and learn from one another. (By contrast, peoples that have been cut off from neighbours and rivals, e.g., the Eskimos, tend to have little or no political culture, but equally have no wars.) It seems clear, then, that, irrespective of their origins and distinguishing characteristics, war and the state have tended to develop under similar competitive conditions and to have given each other probably indispensable support as they developed. And in this sense no one can understand what the state is or what it has accomplished without reference to war. Yet at this point (as already noted in chapter 1) a strange one-sidedness appears in human thought. While the state's internal structure and functions have been the object of some of the most effective efforts of human thought, the idea of war has remained always in the shadowy intellectual background. Its ever-lurking presence, its immense importance, have not been in question. It is the fact that so few general or theoretical questions about it have ever been asked, that demands our attention.

What explains this one-sidedness in men's concern over their contacts with their fellows? One reason is that, although domestic politics are subject to continual friction, interruption and disappointment, it is nevertheless possible to point to certain ideals – justice, harmony and, within limits, liberty – about which there is widespread if not universal human agreement. It is therefore possible at least to argue hopefully about the principles upon which domestic politics should be conducted. But can anything like this be said of war in the general experience of mankind? In General de Gaulle's famous words, war exemplifies to perfection the idea of contingency. It baffles and leaves no time for theoretical understanding. At the same time, it is difficult to see of what use theorizing about it could be. As with love, death, danger and endurance, every sane adult – indeed every imaginative child – recognizes war when he sees or hears about it, without needing to think about its defining characteristics. This has been true of war throughout the whole of what I shall call its 'classic' period, when its characteristic features, rhythms, occasions and consequences were indelibly stamped upon the consciousness of mankind. It was not until the purpose and necessity of war began to be questioned in eighteenth-century Europe, and still more during our own century when developments of war began to threaten the very existence of mankind, that people have begun, belatedly, and for the most part ineffectively, to speculate about its essential nature.

These miscellaneous reflections are not intended to suggest the outlines, or even the possibility, of an overall account or theoretical explanation of the phenomenon of war. They are intended to suggest one answer to the question: why has war retained its virtually unquestioned centrality in the relations of nations for thousands of years? War's diverse roots, major and minor, certainly help to explain its tenacity; but even more important, they help to explain its ostensible unexaminableness. Men have so long assumed that war is as inherent and unavoidable in inter-group relations as are birth and death, joy and sorrow in individual life, or as are the conflicting claims for property and reward in economic production and exchange. It is of the first importance, however, that we should constantly keep in mind the logical insecurity of this assumption. Absence of doubt, worry and puzzlement is no guarantee of intellectual security. (Witness the way in which, in the best-developed sciences, worries about the seemingly simple and unquestionable ideas of *inertia*, of *simultaneity*, of *accumulation* and of *selection*, led to the greatest theoretical achievements of the human intellect.) That the idea of war demands and deserves comparably sustained investigation – that it cannot be allowed to live on unexamined and undisturbed until it destroys humanity – is the basic premiss of this book.

How long, then, did war's 'classic' phase last? Neglecting interruptions of complete social chaos – when it is difficult to decide whether war as such existed or whether it ever stopped – I would say that it stretched from the establishment of war as the main means of settling differences between political units, until approximately two hundred years ago. But why should we treat such an enormous period of time, replete with wars varying so greatly in scale and skill – many of them occurring in areas of the world virtually cut off from and ignorant of each other – as a single phase of warfare? Chiefly, because it rested upon the assumptions which I have just mentioned: that war is one of the great unchangeables in the human scene, that its recurrence has to be accepted – to be endured as a terrible test or to be seized as a golden opportunity; that it neither calls for nor admits of unified theoretical understanding; and that, if not as uniform as the successions of day and night, birth and death and the round of the seasons, the alternation of peace and war, besides being inevitable, is curiously in tune with the other periodicities of human life. In a world in which everything else has its time, war, when not actually occurring, is nevertheless always waiting in the wings. Not surprisingly men's attitude to war has been not unlike that of their primitive forefathers to the most terrible of their gods. There have been times when war's ferocity and indiscriminate destructiveness have made it seem the ultimate evil. But then, as experience seems to prove, *some* people have always survived it and presumably always will survive it, if only by preparing for its return.

Such habitual acceptance of war has rested on expectations which were natural to human groups that were too intellectually constricted to co-operate and yet too interdependent to leave each other alone and too weak to impose domination one on another. Even when innovations in tactics and superiority in manpower and supplies produced what looked like complete and irreversible conquests, they seldom lasted long, so quick has been the spur of military imitation and adaptation whenever group-survival is at stake. Certainly the question whether war might somehow some day be brought to an end – through world conquest by a single power or through rational agreement between near equal powers – seems hardly to have been raised during war's 'classic' phase. Of course there was, in the late Middle Ages and early modern period, much valuable theorizing about the conditions under which it is right to resort to war; but the conclusions of scholastic doctors and Renaissance scholars had no effect on the character and frequency of wars in late medieval and early modern Europe. And the few thinkers, e.g., Erasmus, to whom war between Christian peoples seemed an intolerable scandal, could think of no escape from it except by channelling Christian bellicosity on to the Turks.

A wide variety of factors helped to sustain this acceptance

of war as an indelible feature of the human scene. To mention only a few of these: war was often welcomed as providing a change from the stagnation, miseries, injustices and boredom of peace. It served to strengthen and glamorize certain aspects of the division of labour, between the sexes and between classes and age-groups. It was particularly attractive, during its classic phase, to young men short of other employment and with a taste for adventure, loot and the social advantages which loot commonly brings. And side by side with this, war offered unique opportunities for close companionship and heroic self-sacrifice in the face of danger, as well as honour – especially from women – for dangers endured and overcome. Again, until recently, victory in war has been the main means of acquiring slave-labour, without which no pre-industrial civilizations could have been maintained; and, to move to more specifically political considerations, war has often been an aid to harassed governments, since it channels discontent and disruption at home into hatred of the foreigner, and since the sentiment of national unity is nourished by memories of past victories and even of past defeats in war. Such political uses have their price, however. Most wars leave a legacy of inter-state hatred, bitterness and resentment which it is difficult to shake off. And this legacy is all the more inflammable, the longer and the more desperate and bloody the wars in question have been. Observers of war as different as Thucydides and Tolstoy have pointed out that it eventually drives men to do things which beforehand they would never have dreamed of doing. As it moves to its climax, as the issue between survival and destruction becomes starker, war becomes a great leveller between civilized and barbaric societies; the latter often displaying a genius for war, while the former reveal regressions to barbarism through the chinks in their civilized armour.

There is one further aspect of war in its classic phase which calls for comment. While many wars have been miserably straggling affairs, with starvation and disease causing more casualties than major engagements have done, it has always seemed more agreeable to the human imagination that a war should be ended by a great battle, a supreme test of the valour, man-power, skill and military resources of the contending powers. This is only one way in which war has been dramatized by the human imagination; but it is a way which has affected the judgements of the most sober-minded of statesmen, historians and military leaders. In an activity as generally wasteful as war – in time, effort, life, resources, virtue, hope and personal honour – men find an almost irresistible comfort in thinking that its climax, even when tragic, was nevertheless a great, a dramatically fitting and therefore historically decisive and unforgettable event, worthy of all the efforts and sacrifices that went into it. Wars, men are inclined to think, *ought* to conclude in a great battle, even if in truth they seldom do so. Moreover such wishfulness had more justification in ages of poor communication and transport – when the time, cost and labour of staging a great battle was so great – than we can easily recognize today. Since the Napoleonic age, great commanders have had little difficulty in recruiting and equipping new forces to make good even their most serious disasters. But earlier commanders did not enjoy this advantage. If a great 'set piece' battle was a costly failure the prospect of making good its losses were daunting indeed. Hence the surprising degree to which governments, before the nineteenth century, were liable to be 'thrown' by what appears to us, in retrospect, to have been at least remediable setbacks. The Emperor Augustus was driven to near-madness by the loss of his legions at the hands of Arminius, and no Roman legions were ever to venture so far east again. And no doubt something similar was true of battles which, however unclear their immediate results, have nevertheless been regarded as turning points in European history: those of Tours and Lepanto, for example. Great battles are those which governments and peoples have *felt* to be great. But the all-important fact about even the greatest of battles before the modern age was that none of them was great enough, or involved or threatened such intolerable destruction, as to make men wonder whether war, on such a scale, at such a cost, was a practice which could be continued and expanded into the indefinite future.

What brought the classic phase of war to a close? We need not dispute here about particular events or ideas. The scientific revolution of the sixteenth and seventeenth centuries, the circumnavigation of the globe and the opening-up of world trade, the Cartesian cult of rationality, efficiency and economy in all walks of life, and the humanitarian ideals of the Enlightenment, all played their parts in wearing down the centuries-old assumption that war was one of the great unthinkables – and therefore one of the great constants – of human life. For three very different reasons, however, I find it helpful to take the downfall of Napoleon as the cut-off point of war's 'classic' phase. First, the end of the Napoleonic wars produced a reaction which was a foretaste of that which was to follow the end of World War I: a reaction expressed in the wishful but ineffective slogan 'Never again!' This was given political shape in the nineteenth century's experiments, never very confident or effective, in international organization: the so-called Congress and Conference systems which were intended to settle the outstanding problems of Europe without recourse to war.

More important than these, however, was a positive change in the direction of political and social concerns once the Napoleonic bogy had been removed. The industrial revolution had been well advanced in England in the later decades of the eighteenth century, but it was only after 1815 that political attention began to focus on the social problems to which it gave rise. The most striking feature of these problems was that, as both St Simonites and Marxists observed, they were liable to occur in any European state and were indeed likely to spread across the boundaries of states whatever their traditional social structures or forms of

government might be. They were thus the first international –
as opposed to inter-state – problems of the modern world,
and their complications and confusions were later to
contribute to the total and global character of the world wars
of our century. But in the shorter term their effects were
mainly beneficial. The vision of a world whose problems
would be decided by developments in industry and trade was,
for all its naivety, a much saner one than that of a world
endlessly torn apart by dynastic or nationalist wars. And
when war was again to dominate history in our own century,
it would be war of an entirely different character from any
that had been seen before. It would be a war of whole
peoples and of rival industrial systems. Its destructiveness,
actual and potential, would be beyond all previous experience. It would force even the simplest and shallowest
minds to ask: why should it be? War would indeed have
become a problem.

My third reason for choosing 1815 as the end of war's
classic phase may seem idiosyncratic to a degree. But if I am
right in maintaining that any sane future for mankind
presupposes an entirely new concentration of thought upon
the realities of war, then it is quite possible that the years
between 1815 and 1832 will be remembered, among other
things, for an event which passed unnoticed at the time and
which even today is generally regarded as of interest only to
military specialists. These years saw the writing and the
eventual publication of the first, and to date the only, book
of outstanding intellectual eminence on the subject of war:
Clausewitz's *On War*.[1] It is one of those rare books – Vico's
New Science is another – whose greatness is to be measured
not so much by the conclusions which they establish as by the
tasks which they set themselves: tasks so original that their
authors were not altogether aware of what they had given
birth to. (As Vico seems to have regarded his *New Science* as
a contribution to international jurisprudence rather than to
the philosophy of history, so Clausewitz seems to have
planned his treatise as a manual of instruction for senior

military officers, not as a phenomenology of war, opening up the main obscurities and contradictions in our conception of it.) *On War* has plenty of faults. It was left unfinished and unrevised: it is excessively, and not always consistently, repetitive: its logical apparatus, although impressive, is clumsy and sometimes obscure. Nevertheless it provides the foundation upon which any effective future reflection on war is likely to be based. Clausewitz recognized, better than any philosopher of his own time and perhaps of ours, that the topic of war – and the same holds for the study of most other major human practices – must be appreciated both from a logically analytic and from a broadly historical point of view. Only in this way can we appreciate war as a distinctive form of human activity, understanding the limits of what it can achieve, but also seeing it as a chameleon-like phenomenon, constantly changing and adapting to changes of circumstances which it itself does so much to create. Or, to bring out the peculiar pertinence of this claim for our present discussion, while Clausewitz struggled to extract the logic of war as he had himself experienced it, and did not set himself up as a prophet of the future of war, yet his analyses of what war is and of how it produces its results brings him to the verge of seeing how it was destined to develop. From what he had witnessed and endured in the climax years of the Napoleonic wars – in Germany, in Russia and in the final Waterloo campaign – he could not help concluding that

bounds, which existed only in an unconsciousness of what is possible, when once thrown down are not easily built up again; and that ... whenever great interests are in dispute mutual hostility will discharge itself as we have seen it do in our times.[2]

Clausewitz wrote thirty years too soon to appreciate the effects which industrialization would have on war: the changes which impressed him and which suggested war's continuing escalation in the future were political – the new sense of involvement felt by all classes, first in France as a result of the Revolution, and later in other leading European nations through their resistance to Napoleon. This makes his foresight all the more remarkable.

To bring out the importance, indeed the centrality, of this tension in Clausewitz's military thinking, I take one particularly striking instance. In no way does he show himself to be at once the child and the spokesman of war's classic phase, more than in his insistence on the 'great battle' as the climax and determinant of every serious war. As Sir Michael Howard has pointed out, in the chapters in *On War* which deal with this topic Clausewitz wrote with an emphasis, indeed with a passion, which is matched in no other section of his book. On the other hand, from what he had seen of the French débâcle in Russia, and had heard about popular resistance in Spain, he was for a short time during 1813 a strenuous advocate of the use of guerrilla forces against the French. When he came to write his famous chapter 'The People in Arms' he deals with this topic in a carefully judicious way: successful guerrilla action depends upon the terrain and must be subordinated to major, disciplined and ordered, military action. But again and again in the course of *On War* he returns to the future possibilities of a popular militia, an idea which did not make him any more popular with his Prussian masters. In fine, Clausewitz was uneasily aware that the kind of war about which he knew so much and which he had struggled to delineate with such balanced care, was inherently a thing on the move: and this awareness, although it sometimes confuses, also adds to the intellectual penetration and excitement of his book. If he could not foresee the main direction which that inherent movement was to take, the general thrust and framework of his argument can still help us to recognize and assess its significance. War has to be caught on the move if ever we are to put salt on its tail.

Serious criticism of war as a means of settling international disputes dates back to the middle decades of the eighteenth century. Many (but by no means all) of the leading thinkers of the Enlightenment found war objectionable on grounds both of efficiency and of morality: often provoked by trifles, it seldom achieved anything of consequence. Such criticism first took on systematic and constructive form at the hands of Kant and Bentham, both of whom saw war as an unqualified evil, and peace as a moral imperative; an imperative which was rendered attractive by the promised rewards of un-hampered international trade. During the nineteenth century these highly intellectualist beginnings gained popular support from various quarters: from numerous religious bodies in the wake of the Quakers, from middle-class and working-class political parties (on grounds of free trade in the one case and of international solidarity in the other), while intelligent conservatives had learned how easily wars can lead to political and social upheaval. Altogether, throughout the nineteenth century a wide array of opinions and interests came to be ranged against war in all 'progressive' nations, most notably in the United States, Britain and France, but also in important circles in militaristic Russia and Prussia. War, we might say, had entered the problematic phase.

However, these movements of anti-war opinion and sentiment suffered from two grave weaknesses. Their com-ponent elements never pulled together; on the contrary, they commonly distrusted or despised one another, liberals sniping at conservatives, intellectual radicals at churchmen and so on. Moreover, in the intellectual and rhetorical euphoria of the nineteenth century, anti-war spokesmen too often took their eyes off their proper object: viz. the character and causes of the future wars which they were endeavouring to prevent. The wars they inveighed against were the wars of the mercantile and early capitalist past, not those that were being prepared in the shipyards, railway networks and engineering shops of the western world. Nor was it simply the impact of industrialization on the means of war that was neglected. Nineteenth-century speculation and rhetoric had created the myth of a new pacific, although commercially expansive, Europe. It was widely believed, by Marxists, Comtists and Cobdenists alike, that the great decisions of the future would be taken not on military but on economic grounds, so that international relations were, for the first time in history, about to be demilitarized. However, the sad truth was that during the long peace from 1871 to 1914 the great European nations, despite the caution of conservatives, the international aspirations of liberals and the boasted solidarity of socialists, were developing a submerged passion for war, an emotional and an economic need and readiness for war, as well as a capacity for organizing, supplying and enduring war, of which few if any of their leaders were adequately aware. What were the main ingredients of this long-hidden retrogression into war? They can be collected under two heads.

First, the inherent progressiveness of research science and its seemingly endless capacity to produce continuous improvements in all forms of machinery. This last appeared only gradually in the fields of weaponry and military transport and communication. But by the 1860s the first great naval arms-race had begun. Competition in weaponry and transport soon led to competing plans of war, both offensive and defensive, and by the turn of the century these had given rise to panic in diplomatic circles and to a dangerous xenophobia among the masses of the great industrial powers. The idea had been put around that even in time of peace the greatness of a nation was to be measured by its power to outbuild its rivals, especially in the numbers and firepower of its battleships and in the length and efficiency of its railways. Secondly, the commercial unification of the world immensely enlarged the scale, the stage, the rewards and the motives of wars between industrial nations. From a narrowly European point of view the later nineteenth century seemed a period of comparative peace, but from a global point of view it opened up new possibilities of war as the continuation of European politics on far-off colonial shores. Like the crusades and voyages of discovery which preceded it, the commercial expansion of Europe gave expression to all the egoistic rivalries of its component nations. No one of them could have carried through so immense a task on its own: yet that task demanded a readiness on the part of successive front-runners to ditch, replace or liquidate any competitors who blocked the road to further and speedier exploitation. The commercial unification of the world was something that had to come; it was an inescapable part of the destiny of mankind. But it produced problems more terrible than those which it solved.

Hitherto the European nations had vied with each other for the title of leader of Christendom or conquerors of the New World or establishers of the Raj. But from the late nineteenth century onwards a larger and coarser prize lay open to the leading nations of Europe. To be 'top nation' would now mean to be rulers of the world. It was this idea, however much it might be toned by a poetic cult of honour, which drove thousands of young men to their deaths in 1914 and again – when it achieved its most poisonous form in the fantasies of Hitler – in the 1940s. Empire is, of all forms of political power, the most intoxicating and the most corrupting: and in our century nothing in its reign has become it like the leaving of it by Britain and by France. The tragedy is that the getting of it had involved the leading nations of Europe in the two world wars, in which they lost their place in the collective leadership of the world. Taken together, the two world wars of this century represent, with terrifying repetitive power, the failure of western civilization to cope with the problematic condition of war bequeathed upon it by the nineteenth century. Or, looked at from a different angle, the two world wars represent a deadly advance from the previous problematic condition of war toward an acceptance of its future total, global and genocidal capacities.

Of course, when considered as ordeals – for the individuals, the families, the regions and the nations most affected by them – the two wars differed greatly, as they do when we consider them as military operations, and again, when we consider the kinds of wrong which they were intended to eliminate or contain, and the kinds of leadership, political and military, which they evoked. But these are aspects of the two great wars which reflect the special values and interests of their various participants and our present concern wih them is as two spans of a single bridge that has carried mankind's war-making propensity from the uncertainties of the nineteenth century to the terrifying near-certainties of the nuclear age. To think of the two great wars in this abstract way may seem distasteful, the more so since it suggests that the principal result of World War I was World War II, and that the principal result of World War II was the nuclear menace that still hangs over us all today. But thinking and its results often *are* distasteful, even when they offer the only means of avoiding worse horrors to come.

We are so used to hearing World War I described as the end of an epoch – that of Europe's world hegemony – that it is difficult to envisage it as the first span of a bridge carrying mankind towards a much more terrible future. But the task becomes easier when World War I is considered successively at the levels of popular attitudes, of the new military methods which it involved, and of the quality of the leadership which it called out. On the first score we need only recall the mood of (to us) incomprehensibly innocent euphoria with which, in all the combatant nations, men of different age groups and cultural levels flocked to the colours; and then contrast this with the moods – dazed, bitter, black and in some cases murderous – of those who eventually returned. Next, we should remember the means by which the war was sustained. At the outset the destructive power of the new automatic weapons took generals and statesmen and the public at large by surprise, as later did the horrors of poison gas, submarine warfare and economic blockade. At each stage in this process, the wits of inventors and the endurance of whole populations were to be strained to the limit, to produce an ever further escalation of war towards 'totality'. Finally we may recall the manner of men who found themselves directing the war of August 1914 and compare them with those who were to push it through to its conclusion. Asquith, Viviani and Bethmann-Hollweg were what Gibbon might have called 'decent easy men' in comparison with Lloyd George (the wizard), Clemenceau (the tiger) and Ludendorff (the political mentor of Hitler). At each of these levels World War I afforded proof of Clausewitz's insight: that the higher the stakes in a war between near-equals, the more it becomes a trial by escalation – if necessary beyond all sane and previously credible limits.

In World War II the escalation of the means of violence was at first less noticeable, but once begun and accepted it became even more appalling. As so often, the initial operations resembled those of the previous war, applied this time with more caution. No one in Western Europe wanted a return of the blood-baths of 1914–18. But very quickly, new and more horrifyingly destructive forms of warfare appeared. Aerial bombing was strenuously developed, first as an adjunct to war on land and sea, then as a weapon of economic warfare, and was directed in the end simply upon areas of the densest population. It is in the context of this horrendous strategic development – which left the issue of World War II in doubt until 1945 – that the world-shaking decisions to drop atomic bombs on Japan has to be understood. At the same time, on the East European and Far Eastern fronts war was being conducted with a savagery and with a deliberately indiscriminate ruthlessness that recalled the horrors of the Dark Ages. Nor was it a matter of retrogression only: the worst atrocities in the Far East and in central Eastern Europe shared such sadistic advances as might make sensitive spirits despair completely of mankind. It was therefore altogether fitting that when World War II ended in Europe, no peace treaty was signed. It was widely recognized, with a mixture of trepidation and short-term relief, that with the dropping of America's two atomic bombs, war was already approaching, if it had not already entered, a quite new phase. After the classic and problematic stages, the two world wars had represented the total and global phase, beyond which it could only advance one stage further. Terminally genocidal nuclear war was the prospect with which mankind would now have to live.

We have been facing the nuclear war threat for over forty years and during most of this period the means of waging war have been steadily developed in numbers, accuracy, and inescapable destructiveness. But as yet there has been no nuclear war, either between the super-powers or between one super-power and a minor nuclear power (e.g. Britain) or between a nuclear power and a non-nuclear power (as e.g. in Vietnam or Afghanistan). And in the last few years we have seen the remarkable return on the part of the super-powers to a policy of nuclear disarmament. Their current negotiations, however, do not appear to have envisaged the possibility of renewal of nuclear rivalry and mistrust between them. Nor, apparently, have the super-powers decided how far their nuclear disarmament can be carried with safety in a world in which basic nuclear know-how has become common knowledge: still less, what they can do together to squeeze the poison of nuclear adventurism out of the international system.

In the meantime, wars on a relatively small scale, but often of a horrifying brutality, continue to be fought between industrially undeveloped nations with weapons supplied by the world's leading industrial nations. The super-powers have only rarely take direct part in these wars, and never against each other. They have been content to threaten each other indirectly and at a distance by continually adding to their stocks of both nuclear and conventional weapons, which could be unleashed if certain (far from definite or constant) limits were overstepped by either power. But while they remain in readiness for an increasingly destructive war which they trust will never come, they also seek to gain or defend strategic vantage-points by means of surrogate wars, waged between minor powers, for which the nuclear giants supply not only arms, but cash, military advice and political support. Thus, while actual 'fighting wars' remain a real but minor preoccupation of the super-powers, the avoidance of nuclear-war becomes, in moments of truth, their most urgent, if still far from safely manageable, concern. Recognition of the fact that it *is* their common concern, and that it is something which no other powers but themselves can do very much about, sticks, however, not in their throats but somewhere in their higher cerebral centres: the result of an inheritance of assumptions about the rule of war in international relations from which neither as yet can shake itself free.

Let me now try to bring together the main points that are raised by this very rough survey of our received conception of war. It is a conception which, both because of its veiled and deceptive history and because of the opposing tensions which propel and retard it, seems destined to cause intellectual confusion, leading on to cynicism, complacency or despair. And yet the idea of war has its own distinguishing rhythms and limits which can be charted, and which suggest the possibility of its eventual control. Once the effort to survey it synoptically becomes habitual, and the mists and quagmires of *not* thinking about it recede if only a little way; once this debilitating quandary is felt as a positive puzzle and the puzzle takes the outline of a problem, then there is no reason why this long uncut chapter in the human story should not become as intellectually accessible as any other. Of course there are obstacles, in the form of obdurate thought-habits, to be overcome. No sooner had the *practice* of war become established between human societies than the *idea* of war took its place among the great and vague, the recurrent but ineradicable, determinants of human life. And although wars have been subject to continual change, in form, scope, purpose and destructiveness, they have continued to occupy the same high ground among mankind's emotional concerns, always too fearsomely close to that of national survival to admit of cool and lucid examination. Indeed it has seemed as if war was something too big – at once too permanent and too Protean – for men to think about with any hope of understanding or controlling it.

And then almost suddenly, and as one of the characteristic ventures of our western civilization, people began to question the permanence and necessity of war, at the very time when its modes and means of operation were revealing a destructive potential far beyond all previous dreams and fears of mankind. How were these two assaults – from entirely opposite directions – upon traditional attitudes to war to be assimilated and developed together by minds quite unaccustomed to thinking about war in general terms? More particularly, what sense and what grounds of hope could people find in a phase of history that embraced two world wars leading into a Cold War which, if it had once been ignited, would have reduced our civilization to rubble? Faced by these thought-paralysing questions, we are all of us inclined to dither between two positions which serve as excuses for our inadequacy. One is that our 'classic century of war' has been the result of the unbalancing effect of the technological revolutions which have rendered war 'total'. The other is that no matter how ingenious and sophisticated men become they remain at heart unthinkingly self-assertive and absurdly suggestible savages. Neither of these answers does anything to stimulate intellectual initiative or to stiffen moral backbones. They are alike, however, in neglecting a line of thought which, if not optimistic, at least suggests a future with which we can grapple with a will.

This is to the effect that the incomparable scientific advances of our age are not the cause of our total and potentially terminal wars, they have simply served to release and reveal a key characteristic of war, its inherent tendency to escalate, which had previously been concealed and retarded by the persistent paucity of its means. R.G. Hawtry came close to the mark with his brilliant epigram 'The principal cause of war is war itself.' But he would have done better to specify the particular feature of war which not only typifies its operation in every important instance but links every war to those which have preceded it. War's tendency to escalate is at first blush so obvious that nobody (before Clausewitz) stopped to consider it. But it has worked its way out with a mole-like persistence, forcing itself upon men's consciousness and demanding its price: to be recognized for what it is, as man's probable destroyer or as the warning which may drive him to divert and control his war-making propensities.

Notes

1   Karl von Clausewitz's great work, *On War*, was published posthumously by his wife in 1832. There are at least three good English translations: I have used the one by Michael Howard and Peter Paret (1976), published by Princeton University Press.
2   *On War*, Bk VIII, Ch. 6, B.

4. War: an inherently cumulative process

What is the purpose, and what is the justification, of speaking of war's *inherent* tendency to escalate? Is it to say anything more than that the stronger our opponent proves to be, the harder we have to fight to defeat him? This last would be perhaps all that we would mean if we could confine our talk and thought about war to this, that or the other particular war, i.e., to war considered distributively. But we also think of war in a collective and, in some degree, a cumulative sense: comparable in its duration and development to the practices of agriculture and building, of marriage and hospitality, of story-telling and record-keeping, and of the education of the young and the burial of the dead. What I shall be urging in this chapter is that war, thus conceived, has involved from the outset a tendency to expand or escalate; and that it is this inherent but by no means all-determining tendency which gives to war, in its collective sense, such intelligibility as it possesses. It is impossible to think of any particular war without a half-thought about the wars which preceded it, and at least a quarter-thought for the wars which might follow it or which it may, with luck, have prevented.

In arguing to this effect I am by implication attacking all those who have maintained, often explicitly, that war is essentially either a means or an expression or a by-product of other more creative social forces, tensions and conflicts. In particular I am arguing against those who see in war's recent horrific escalations into global, total and potential nuclear wars a simple and unfortunate coincidence of mankind's inveterate habit of fighting with its recently acquired capacity to direct and control the most powerful forces of Nature. The main point that I want to put over is that the unholy marriage of war and science-based technology in our century has been no mere coincidence. (Still less, of course, has it been something foreseeable.) Like all potent marriages, it has involved a wooer and a wooed, between which (allowing for a certain amount of role-reversal) the great positive advances in war have been made: with war, throughout most of its history, giving the leads, and with science and industry responding, by piecemeal contributions at first but latterly with increasing eagerness, until they have endowed war with its potentially terminal form.

How this process, which we have all seen presented in concrete form in the history of our century, is best presented from a logical point of view, so as to avoid both clever and stupid misunderstandings, is a question that can be left to philosophical logicians. The key terms in which it is posed – tendency, necessity, conditionality, inherence and essence, cumulation, escalation and apogee – are all notoriously hazy and slippery. But they can be kept under control so long as the central thesis is held firmly in mind. My thesis is that war has become, in our age, what it always had in itself to become since its establishment as one of the characteristic practices of mankind: a means of settling inter-societal differences and conflicts which admits of becoming more and more violent to the point where violence passes, irreversibly, into self-destruction. . . . So let us try to see how this has happened.

It seems clear that, once war was invented and recognized for what it is, news of it must have spread like wildfire. Since it threatened the persistence of any human group, every group had to be prepared for it, which usually meant being prepared to take part in it. But the speed with which war spread does not explain its intensification in respect of destructive power. Many human practices have spread fast and wide without any comparable increase in their intensity. What accounts, then, for the cumulative character of warfare, clearly manifested at different periods of its history, but most obviously and threateningly during the last hundred odd years? At first the answer seems simple. War has expanded in scale, range and intensity because it is inherently a *competitive* activity. Few, if any, peoples engage in wars just for the fun of it. Usually they fight – or believe that they are fighting – for survival, or for the necessary means of survival, or because they are frightened of being dispersed, enslaved or put to the sword. For any or all of these reasons, they believe that they must possess, or at least appear to possess, as much military strength as any possible opponent. So competition for survival requires, from the outset, a readiness to enlarge and intensify the means and the will for war. But, in addition, success in war usually makes for an expansion of the numbers, resources and ambitions of the victors, so that they are in a position to put up a stronger defence or to launch stronger attacks upon ever greater enemies. Thus general readiness for war easily turns into preparation for ever bigger and more costly wars, and war acquires its cumulative character.

This account is persuasive up to its last step, when the tendency of war to escalate is attributed to the results of successful wars – i.e., to the increases in strength and power which they bring to the victor. But, although there is important truth in this claim, it neglects another possibility, viz. that some of the roots of war's cumulative character lie in the act of warring itself, whether successful or unsuccessful. Is it not possible that war has its own escalating dynamism? The sense of war as something that masters men, something into which they can be trapped and which grips and directs their actions in ways that could not be foreseen, is familiar to all those who have experienced it most sharply or reflected on it most deeply. But before we engage with this question more deeply it will be useful to take a brief glance at our ordinary ideas of competition and appreciate what a very peculiar form of competition war is.

In all competition men strive against one another in pursuit of some object or end, which each would like to win entirely for himself even if he has eventually to compromise and share it. Political parties, in a democracy, compete for government; businessmen compete for a particular order or for sustained custom in a certain line of commerce; advocates compete to win over the mind of a jury; athletes strive for acknowledged superiority, as in different ways do artists and scientists; the lover strives in a variety of ways to be preferred above all others in the eyes of his beloved. There are of course immense differences in the styles and methods of these different instances of competition. But there are two ways in which those who engage in them stand relatively together, in contrast to those who compete by means of war. First, there is an unmistakable difference between the characteristic interactions of the competitors in all the above-mentioned instances and the interactions which make up war. Secondly, there is a notable similarity, in all the cases just cited, in respect of the part played by third parties in determining which of the competitors will succeed: a similarity which is almost entirely missing in the case of war. Let us take up these two differences in turn.

(1) Competition in politics, business, the law, the arts and sciences, as well as in love, can be intense and bitter and may end in violence and tragedy. But such results are far from characteristic. Economists have pointed out how deper-sonalized most business competition becomes as market-mechanisms are perfected: and somewhat similar considerations apply in the other cases which I have listed. Rivals at the bar or in science – or even in the arts – can show sincere respect for their rivals' skills and achievements; the life of politics is occasionally brightened by generous gestures of recognition between outstanding opponents; and, in spite of jealousy, rivals in love can remain firm friends. But in the

case of war the simplest horse-sense tells us that we must treat the enemy as an enemy to be killed or disarmed and put out of action so far as the present conflict is concerned. The vulgar demand that the enemy shall be 'wiped out' expresses perfectly the brute antagonism, the all-or-nothing competiveness of war.

(2) This contrast is heightened when we consider the part played by third parties in most forms of competition – by the voting public, by potential customers and clients, by informed critical opinion and the judgements of official umpires and referees. The general effect of such third parties is clear. It is to moderate and civilize the conduct of the competitors: to keep their rivalry within bounds, to remind them that defeat need not mean disaster, that the market-place is wide open and that tomorrow is another day. The aim of most competition is thus to displace rather than to destroy one's rivals. It is obvious, however, that in war such considerations have virtually no place. The conduct of war is unique in its almost exclusive concentration upon *the enemy*. Even when he is purposely being misled, his every move has to be registered if not resisted; and eventually he must be disabled or destroyed. Such concentration is inevitably of a most blinkered kind – which explains why war is often such a wasteful process. While the enemy is being destroyed, perhaps at an appalling cost, the very object for which the war is being fought may have disappeared or have altered out of recognition. This peculiarity – this deadly simplicity – of war seems to have escaped the notice of those theorists who maintain that war is only one form among many of mankind's inherent competitivenesses, and that in future the struggle between nations may be conducted in terms of trade or fashion or competitive sport or whatever – a possibility to which we are blinded by the destructive capacity of the weapons which science has recently put into our hands. But this way of thinking fails to explain why the science-based technology of the modern industrialized nations should have been poured into ever more accurate and irresistible weapons

of destruction. Did this happen because human societies are fundamentally self-destructive? Or because they have been re-brutalized by industrialization? I see no reason to think so. Industrialization has inflicted new and terrible wounds but none that matches those of mankind's long and relatively powerless childhood, without remedy against natural calamity, starvation, disease, ignorance and fear. If we want to understand what we have been doing with our recently granted technological opportunities we must look in a quite different direction. Science-based technology has simply done for mankind, quickly and continuously for a century or so, what a succession of sporadic discoveries – from the war-chariot to the movable cannon – had been doing, jerkily and intermittently, for centuries. These discoveries show us that war has an appetite for innovation as much as for blood – an appetite which calls out for continually new forms of destructiveness. But, as we have seen, the advantages of such revolutionary advances in warfare have usually been short-lived. As a rule, they are copied by those against whom they have been proved, and war soon returns, although at a higher level of destructiveness, to its typical condition: an armed struggle between communities, each of which is aware of the risks involved and therefore braces itself by putting *more*, in some relevant sense, into a struggle to the death than its opponent has the wit or the will to do.

Here we are re-treading Clausewitzian ground. And without burdening ourselves with Clausewitz's terminology or with the peculiarities of the wars which he had studied most closely – those of Frederick the Great and of Napoleon – we can here usefully reconsider the main tenets of his teaching.

Clausewitz's doctrine of war

Clausewitz's exposition of the concept of war proceeds dialectically, and it is far from easy to decide whether its opposed theses are ever quite satisfactorily reconciled. The first thesis is that war, in all its manifestations, is essentially a struggle which tends to escalate and whose characteristic results are to be explained in terms of escalation. He seems to have regarded this claim as so obviously true as hardly to need elaboration or defence, although, as we shall see, it demands and admits of a good deal of both. Clausewitz's second thesis is that observation and history provide numerous counter-examples to his first thesis. Many wars are brought to a close before they have escalated in any notable way, while others peter out inconclusively. Clausewitz's normative teaching, however, has seemed to some of his expositors to effect a reconciliation between these two positions. War, he insists, is a serious matter, and no state should ever engage in it or continue with it except for a serious purpose. From this point of view war appears as an instrument of politics and this explains why, instead of escalating to the absolute limit of their means, governments often decide to break off a war, even when it promises brilliant results, for the sake of wider political interests. When he writes in this vein (when he explains why Napoleon signed the Treaty of Campo Formio for example), Clausewitz is conforming to the power politics of his age. Nevertheless his first position, that war has an inherent tendency to escalate and that this is the condition of its success, is never wholly relinquished. What is the reason for this crucial duality in thinking?

There seem to me to have been two reasons, one formal, obvious and unobjectionable, and, arising out of this, a second reason which is darker, more obscure and deeply prophetic. First of all, then, *On War* is a book about war, not about the political conditions and justifications of war. It is notable that throughout the book, in spite of his lucid and penetrating views on the politics of his age, Clausewitz nowhere takes it upon himself to advise governments about the kinds of political purpose for which war can most reasonably be engaged. In this sense he *assumes* the primacy of politics. But he sees this primacy as a matter of broad decisions – to go to war, to withdraw from it, or, more rarely, to deflect its course in some radical way. Within these limits, and subject to these political decisions, lies the field of the art of war, with its own guiding principles: in essence almost blindingly simple, but in their applications almost infinitely variable and difficult. The first of these principles is the apparent platitude that, when a commander is charged with any military task, no matter how qualified or conditional, he can discharge it only through his ability – actual or threatened or reported – to 'best' his opponent, i.e., to demonstrate his superiority whether locally or in a general theatre of operations. The successful commander is the one who achieves superiority, against an opponent who is trying to do exactly the same thing, at the decisive place or moment. And thus the victor in war is the winner in the gambling game of escalation.

Thus far it would seem that the two poles of Clausewitz's dialectical treatment of war *can* be reconciled. War *is* the continuation of state-policy with the addition of other means; but these means have their own very distinctive character. Politics is the producer and even the stage manager, but once the play has started – and until it is called off – all eyes are on the actors, and their special tasks strengths and talents. But now comes a further complication. The overall control of war by politics is never complete – never completely clear or completely sure. A government which seeks to secure certain sanely limited political ends by military means may find that these involve consequences which could not be foreseen. Not only may the required military means prove to be unexpectedly costly; they may actually lead to the acceptance of larger and more difficult political objectives than those which inspired the original venture. (This, Clausewitz believed, is what happened to Napoleon in his Russian campaign.) Either of two developments may follow. We may have the spectacle of an absurd war, in which a crazy leader engages in military adventures far beyond the resources at his command. Or, sometimes, a government, its armies and its people, may risk everything, sanely and realistically, to fight their way out of a terrible predicament into which they have fallen. In this case we shall have what Clausewitz called 'war in its absolute form' and what we know today as 'total war'. Government, people, commanders and fighting men will be stretched to the limit; political aims and military means will be fused almost indistinguishably, with horrific but perhaps epoch-making results. For Clausewitz, war in its absolute form is not simply a colossal blood-letting exercise. It is what war is 'really' like because it is the ultimate point at which all serious wars are liable to arrive.

Clausewitz's unusually intense and varied experience of war helps to explain this part of his military thinking. He had begun his military career (as a boy of twelve) under the rigid, narrow discipline of the Prussian system. But he had then seen the Prussian armies collapse before the patriotic fervour and massed columns of the French, first under Revolutionary leadership then under Napoleon. This experience helped him to appreciate the different components that can contribute to military superiority. Later he had taken part in the Russian resistance to Napoleon, and had helped to organize popular resistance to the French in Prussia's Baltic provinces, before he returned to normal military duties (as Chief of Staff in Thielman's corps) in the 1815 campaign. He had thus seen land-warfare in a great variety of aspects, conducted with an intensity perhaps never previously matched in European history. This largely explains his central conviction: that, in order to appreciate the distinctive task and effectiveness of war, one must consider it in its absolute form, or at full throttle with everything subordinated to the achievement of victory. All serious wars are decided by superior strength, whether actually deployed and demonstrated or irresistibly threatened. But in most wars (and particularly those which Clausewitz regarded as 'half-wars') the specific factor of military superiority is liable to be obscured in a medley of other considerations – seasonal, geographical, medical, economic, diplomatic. 'Half-wars' Clausewitz admits, have played an important part in political history; but among models and principles of military action they have no place whatsoever.

This conviction on Clausewitz's part points back to the originally educational aim of his book: to be a manual for advanced military studies. As such it could not usefully look back very far, at least as regards the particularities of military education; hence its concentration on the wars of Frederick and Napoleon. Nor could it usefully look far forward into the unpredictable military future. And again it was too much to expect young ambitious military officers to devote long and hard thought to war's essential nature, whether static or evolving. This partly explains the unresolved duality of Clausewitz's military thinking: on the one hand his insistence that war in its absolute form shows us the essential truth about war, and on the other hand his insistence that in all circumstances war must remain the instrument of state policy. The soldier has his job and his art, with its relatively simple principles; the statesman has his job with its ostensibly more fluid and complicated principles. In every war the two are conjoined; in every great war we see them combined, indeed almost interfused, in an astonishing way. It is only natural, however, that there should be, in any war, some degree of friction or misfit between the demands and needs of the two. Hence, it could plausibly be argued, the uneasiness which Clausewitz shows in and through his accounts of their co-operation. And hence, it could be argued again, his frequent returns to this topic, as though there were still something to be said about it which he had never quite managed to say. But in this he was almost certainly deluded, obsessed by a would-be philosopher's mare's-nest. There is nothing particularly deep or difficult – or revealing – about our received conception of war. War is, logically as well as physically, a rough-and-ready as well as a brutal and bloody affair. And philosophers and military men have been, for once, at one and right in refusing to waste their time in worrying about its essential nature.

And yet, against this easy and natural explanation of the central duality in Clausewitz's military thinking, there are two considerations which have escaped the attention of both the philosophers and the soldiers. First, war is not simply a succession of incidents in which each side seeks to establish its superiority by force of arms. War exists, collectively and cumulatively, as a human practice and institution, jerkily but persistently growing in complexity and destructive power and exercising an immense influence, not only destructive, upon almost every other aspect of organized human life. Secondly, the capacity to escalate one's effort in order to achieve superiority, which appears to decide the result of individual duels and particular military engagements and wars, largely explains, although less directly, the changing overall character of war as an almost universal human practice. The fights and duels of mankind have had, as their long-term effect, an ever-rising level of destructiveness in the preparations for war. It was, therefore, no accident that Clausewitz's book should begin with the image of two wrestlers, each trying to throw his opponent so that he can put up no further resistance, and should end with a guarded prophecy that the future wars of Europe would surpass, in scope and violence, the wars of Napoleon. And it was no philosophical pretentiousness on Clausewitz's part which forced him to return again and again to the two faces of war which haunted his memory and guided his intellectual imagination. If ever a man had a philosophical task forced upon him by his life's experience, it was he.

What Clausewitz failed to do, no doubt out of intellectual modesty, was, in the first place, to present a general exposition of the concept of war: an exposition both analytical and historical which would present the idea of escalation as at once the main motor of every particular military success and also the main motor of war's overall development as an institution. Had Clausewitz been writing some fifty years later he would no doubt have cast his ideas within some kind of evolutionary framework in which every important battle or war would play the role of a variation helping to decide the future life-forms of war. But secondly, and again through lack of a biological framework, he failed to ask himself whether the immense escalation of war which he had witnessed in his life-time could possibly continue unchecked into the indefinite future. Within a hundred and twenty years of his death, industrial technology based on nuclear physics had shown war's capacity to destroy the world. Obviously Clausewitz could not foresee anything resembling this development. But he might have been expected to consider the abstract possibility that war, when escalated to the limit of the resources – physical and moral – of any people or civilizations, might result in its total dissolution: as the Paraguayan war of the 1860s was said almost to have done, leaving that helpless country destitute of all but infants and old men and women. Clausewitz was intensely aware of the changing character of war: but it did not occur to him to raise the question of the limits of its changes, nor to consider seriously the possibility of war's virtual disappearance through a general appeasement of international relations. Still less did he envisage the possibility – central to Kant's philosophy of peace and war – that the threat of war's intolerable escalation would eventually provide governments and nations with a new motive for devising other methods of settling their international differences.

Behind these gaps in Clausewitz's military thinking there lies an even simpler one. As I remarked earlier, the tendency of wars to escalate seemed to him so obvious as to call for no detailed or logically progressive explanation, showing how escalation provides the central thread in any overall concept of war. It seems to me, however, that such a demonstration has, in our time, become essential if we are to learn how to command war in thought and to control it in practice. I cannot offer a complete vindication of the central assumption of Clausewitz's doctrine of war, but I am convinced that its main outlines must be as follows.

Let us begin by asking: what distinguishes a fight between two men from a fight between two animals – birds or dogs or deer. The natural answer is that in the latter case not only the causes but the actual business or operation of fighting seems to be entirely instinctual; it contains no intellectual – or descriptive or symbolic – component, in the form of ideas of the why and the wherefore, or of the progress and prospects of the engagement, for all that its outcome may be of the greatest biological moment to the creatures involved. (Animals do not think about what they are doing, although they know superbly well how to do it; just as they do not talk about what they have done or are going to do.) It may be objected to this, that the same is true of many if not most fights between men or boys. So let us ask: what makes a fight between two men a serious fight as opposed to the throwing of a few unruly punches or a piece of horse-play that goes too far? A plausible answer is that a fight is serious when each combatant is fighting with the definite idea or intention of winning, i.e., of destroying his opponent's capacity to keep on fighting. This may sound platitudinous, but if examined closely it does reveal something which we may already know but whose implications we certainly seldom follow through. Fighting to destroy an opponent's capacity to keep on fighting presupposes that his strength and will have a breaking-point – if only we could reach it. And this idea has as its obverse the even vaguer idea of at least one further increment of effort on our part which – if only we can make it – will make him break. To call this an 'idea' may appear to be an absurd piece of over-intellectualization. Certainly it is only rarely a 'good idea' in the sense of being or containing a new intelligent insight as to how the fight can be won. What I am here concerned with is more in the nature of a handle or a foothold for morale than a signpost to victory in the struggle (although we should here remember Clausewitz's wry comment that the use of the utmost physical force does not necessarily exclude the co-operation of intelligence). It is, however, that postulate or belief which gives to every serious fight its dramatic and potentially heroic quality no matter how blindly animal and bullying it may appear to be. For it contains the seed of the never wholly expungeable human belief that, when there is a struggle between near or apparent equals, victory goes to the 'better man', i.e., to the combatant who puts out and puts into the struggle more of what it takes – more force, more stamina, more concentration, more frenzy – in order to reach his opponent's breaking-point. This is what distinguishes a serious fight from a mere spasm or gesture of fury, or from a trial of strength that is a mere joke or is seen to have been a silly mistake.

And yet, of course, this inner or subjective reality of any serious fight does not decide its outcome. The ideas of the opponent's breaking-point and of our own next – and perhaps last – increment of effort are not sufficient to explain what actually happens. This may indeed have been as good as decided in advance by all manner of outside or objective factors of which neither combatant is aware, but which an uninvolved spectator (like a professional commentator at a boxing-bout) could well have observed: for instance, certain facts about the physique or training or technique of either fighter or about the setting of the fight which favoured one party rather than the other or, above all, by the sheer quantitative factors of reach and weight and speed. Because of this, a shrewd observer would almost certainly give us a far fuller and more illuminating account of the progress of the fight than either contestant could do. And yet, no matter how much more informative such an account might be, it would still be predicated upon the primitive recognition of the fight as a fight aimed at victory and sustained by the ideas of the opponent's breaking-point and of the last increment of effort which can achieve this. For without this primitive ideational core there would be no fight to appreciate and explain.

What, then, is the value of this 'incremental' interpretation of fighting? Does it add anything to the platitude that, in order to defeat B, A must exert such superior force upon him as to prevent his further resistance to A's will? The suspicion that it does not accounts for the view of some quite serious military thinkers that Clausewitz's central teaching is vacuous. Its value, however, is two-fold. It enables us to see the linkage, and at the same time to appreciate the distance, between the simplest acts of fighting and that fantastic transformation of fighting which is modern war. There is little difficulty in tracing this linkage through the disorderly affrays of gang-warfare to the smallest military engagements. In both these cases it is the spirit of group resistance and defiance – an extension of the individual's command of his own increments of effort – which at once engages our attention. It is when we come to the immense mass actions of modern war that the 'objective' factors of numbers, equipment, organization and supply appear to dominate the scene. A first very one-sided recognition of this point was achieved by those eighteenth-century military theorists who envisaged war as a kind of chess – played of course with flesh and blood pieces – on which success depended on the preparations, calculations and adjustments of mathematically sophisticated commanders and ministers of war. The wars of Napoleon (and Clausewitz's interpretations of them) gave the lie to such futilities. Calculation and organization are of course indispensable in all war: but only with a view to injecting and unleashing superior force at the critical place and time. In every serious military engagement, as much as in any individual struggle, it is the readiness to escalate, it is the injection of *more*, more of whatever is needed and whatever it takes, that carries the day.

Now if this is the great rule of military practice, should we not expect the military plans and preparations of governments to follow the same rule? Should not *potential* superiority over all foreseeable enemies and rivals be continually sought and continually developed? But to suggest this would be to attribute to nations and governments a militarily obsessional consistency which, with all their other faults, they very rarely exhibit. Man is indeed a war-making animal, but he is also an animal that tires of war and of war-preparation as well as of other things. Intelligent governments know what is needed to win wars – as and when they arise. But that is a quite different thing from being ready and able to meet that need, year in and year out against all imaginable comers. And of course the overall history of war shows that its expansion has always been a matter of fits and starts, stagnations and even regressions, suddenly reanimated by technological discoveries or by the ruthless exploitation of previously neglected chances. One thing, however, gives an all-important kind of conditional continuity to this outwardly disjointed history: namely, the constant readiness of governments and of military men to seize upon any new and more effective means that will enable them to deal with – to withstand, or defeat and lay down the law to – an intolerable enemy. It is this ingrained habit and hope of military thinking, as progressive in its own way as the thinking of businessmen or of scientists, that is at the heart of the war-culture which we have all inherited. For several thousand years that culture has instilled the belief that there are no lengths of destructiveness to which a government is not entitled, and, more, is not obliged to go to preserve or advance the interests of its people. Today, as I have said, we tend to attribute the apogee of this process to relatively external and independent causes, in particular to the recent astonishing developments in industrial and information technologies. What I want to emphasize, however, as a corrective to this temptingly easy excuse, is that the whole thrust of our war-culture across the ages has been *towards* this apogee. Our twentieth-century technology has simply permitted us to realize the dreams of military triumph and hegemony which have been nurtured down the centuries by the delusion that, no matter how much the destructive power of war may expand, it will remain the ultimate means of defending and advancing national interests.

Thus war's inherent tendency to escalate, rooted as it is in men's simplest acts of fighting, finds its fullest expression in the nuclear anxieties of our age. Although suggested by the teachings of Clausewitz, it has found in our twentieth-century predicament a more terrible endorsement than he could possibly have foreseen. In its simplest manifestations it is so central to human collective endeavour as to seem almost instinctive; but in its final manifestations – or as we face it today – it is evidently and mercifully conditional upon a wide variety of factors. There is nothing fatalistically necessary or predictable about its further or final developments. Yet it is of the first importance that we learn how to think about it, not simply as one abstract possibility among thousands of others which are too remote or unlikely to occupy the thoughts of active politicians. (For example, the possibility that unparalleled disturbances in remotest space are already threatening our galaxy, or that viruses in process of natural creation or scientific manufacture are about to destroy life on the planet.) That is why, in the previous paragraph, I wrote of 'the war-culture which we have all inherited'. This idea seems to me as serviceable as – and in many respects less objectionable than – the idea of Original Sin was to our forefathers. So let me elaborate on it a little.

Clausewitz in a famous passage insists that political relations – contacts, communications etc. – do not stop between states the moment that they declare war: at least potentially they continue, and await renewal. It is much more important, however, to remember that war-planning and preparation do not stop with the signing of peace between previously warring nations. In the history of post-Renaissance Europe, and today in world history, a whole gamut of political attitudes and practices, central to the life of nations, has had the effect of inclining men's minds towards accepting war as the indispensable defence of national interests. This tendency has become all the more marked and all the more dangerous in our age of rapid technological competitiveness and improvements, one of whose side-effects is an open market in cast-off weaponry and (one cannot but suspect) in odd bits of nuclear gadgetry and know-how. No one can say at what exact point of time adherence to the assumptions of our war-culture would make it certain that we are about to destroy our civilization. But the fact that that question can be raised and needs to be kept at the forefront of our minds, properly casts a shadow and induces a shiver as we contemplate the future of mankind. Our participation in a slide which could well lead to universal disaster has been unwitting, and to some extent unwilling. But that does not lessen our responsibility for controlling and diverting it.

5 War and power

Not only has war a tendency to expand 'vertically', i.e., in intensity and in the scale of its destructiveness, it also expands 'horizontally', i.e., in its influences upon other spheres of human life, particularly upon politics. There can also be influences in the opposite direction, as when political or religious enthusiasm inspires an army with extraordinary discipline and zeal. My present concern, however, is with the former tendency, viz. the *militarization* of political thought and action in the international field.

As we saw in chapter 2, international politics tends to oscillate between two poles, the power-political and the idealist or legalist, with the former dominating whenever serious issues arise. I also claimed that power-politics, on the most generous view, has been at best a kind of braking mechanism in the development of inter-state relations, whose main directions and drives have been dictated by war or the threat of war. It requires little argument, however, to show that, whatever justification power-politics as thus conceived may have had in the past, its *raison d'être* has been undercut in the nuclear age. No one in his or her senses can today countenance the claim that war should be reserved for the speedy and effective resolution of major differences between nations. And yet the super-powers, throughout the years of the Cold War, continued to talk and act as if the political attitudes which they had inherited from more primitive ages were irreplaceable. More generally, mankind appears to be afflicted by a maladjustment between the kinds and quantities of weapons of war now at its disposal and the purposes for which weapons (of a hitherto far less fatal destructiveness) have been invented and deployed in the past. Engels, following Hegel, invoked what he called 'the law of the transformation of Quantity into Quality' to explain apparent 'jumps' in both social and natural processes. Somewhat similarly, it could be argued, there are human practices whose ostensible 'improvements' have the effect of drastically changing their point and purpose for the societies which have developed them. War, in our century, has manifestly become one of these, as have (although with less immediately threatening effects) many industrial processes and many of the mechanisms of exchange. Now, while such changes in respect of point and purpose can easily be understood once they are pointed out, they can be painfully difficult to adjust to in practice.

The habits of thought which dominate international relations were laid down, unfortunately, long before the days of Hegel and Engels. They have thus a seemingly timeless authority and force which it is not easy to dismiss. What could be more arresting, but also more patently false, than Machiavelli's dictum that 'a prince should have no other object or thought, nor acquire skill in anything, except to make war'? Thomas Hobbes was impelled by similar intellectual motives when he described relations between states as subscribing to 'the state of nature', i.e., 'a war of all against all'. More recently, in his early short work *Power Politics*, Martin Wight underlined this view with a literary incisiveness surpassing that of either of these past masters. 'A power', he wrote, 'becomes a Great Power by a successful war against another Great Power, as the head-hunters of Borneo enter into manhood by taking their first head.' Again, 'Great Power status is lost, as it is won, by violence. A great power does not die in its bed'. 'Great Powers tend to decrease in number and to increase in size.' And finally he quotes with approval the apothegm, 'Diplomacy is potential war'.[1]

Liberal internationalists very properly reject these views as over-simplified, morally repugnant and outmoded in our partially unified world. But their rejection of them has rested on an equally simplistic assumption: that international relations can proceed along lines suggested by the domestic politics of modern liberal democracies. The fallacy of this way of thinking is obvious. In the face of any marked innovation or conflict of interests within an established state, the parties involved are inclined to moderation and com-promise because of their inherited habits of co-operation and obedience. A domestic opponent has often been and may well become again a useful client, customer or friend. But a foreign opponent is first seen − or felt − as a potential aggressor and conqueror. With the former, most conflicts are about some advantage or convenience; with the latter they may well be conditions of national survival. In fine, liberal internationalists ignore how difficult it is for different political societies to recognize, or to show any interest in, each other's power-needs and power-possibilities, until these present themselves in the form of a challenge which betokens or openly threatens war. This attitude is, no doubt, narrow and short-sighted. But until they abandon it liberal inter-nationalists will remain unwitting but dangerous self-deceivers.

These considerations suggest the need for a drastic revision, or at least extension, of the idea of power as manifested in international relations. In this field it is very important to distinguish two aspects of power; the first of which predominates when we think of how power is sustained and preserved in society, and the second when our concern is with how it is exercised or expended. To speak in very rough and ready terms, although the two aspects of power are always to some extent complementary, the first is the capacity to pull and to hold people *together*, the second is the capacity to push other people *around*. The first aspect of power commands, controls and gives cohesion to what, without it, would be merely a chaos of separate individual wills. The second aspect of power compels and constrains, if necessary by scattering or destroying whatever opposes it. The great weakness of most discussions of political power is to assume that the first of these aspects is merely a precondition of the second; whereas it would be truer to say that the second is only one exercise, although a very important exercise, of the first. Or, to put this point more exactly: power in both its aspects is a multi-purpose affair, but its second aspect is the more specific of the two. Some degree of commanding, controlling and cohesive power in society is a necessary prerequisite of all compellent or constraining power. But this is by no means the only function and value of commanding or cohesive power which pulls and holds people together in a wide variety of social enterprises: in the forming of a new party or association, or church, crusade or business, for example.

Two affinities of this first aspect of power are worth keeping in mind. First, up to a point, its effects are comparable to those of beauty or personal charm. They operate beyond the control of reason if not always against the dictates of reason, and they frequently deceive. But an individual's commanding and controlling power differs from beauty in that it is usually recognized and measured by the size and strength of the group or organization which it commands. The powerful individual and his following are, in varying degrees, interdependent: they feel what they owe to him, and he knows what he owes to them. And to this we must add – and here there is no parallel with beauty or personal charm – that one essential element in an individual's commanding power is his capacity, not only to keep his followers in line without treading on their toes, but to deal firmly with anyone who tries to intrude into his domain or to confuse or divide his followers or to challenge his authority over them.

The second affinity that is worth mentioning here is that between an individual's commanding power and the kind of power which is attributed to great scientific ideas and theories. These not only gather up and explain a wide variety of previously unordered phenomena, they very quickly command all but universal agreement from competent judges of the problems in question. Everything and everyone seems to fall in with them. And yet, of course, the persuasive authority of even the most powerful theories – those of a Newton or a Darwin for example – does not last for ever.

In the international field the two aspects of power which I have distinguished usually stand in relations of close and balanced complementarity. Either form of power – the commanding or the compellent – may appear to be all-important in a particular instance, but its dependence upon the other form soon becomes evident. Thus the need to dispel an invader will commonly call out a spirit of national cohesion which will easily pass, in turn, into a spirit of self-assertion and compellence. Or, to look at the matter from another angle, even so brutally compellent a power as the Ottoman Empire did not depend simply upon its capacity for war and conquest, which would have been impossible without its support system of religious indoctrination, and its skilful organization of agriculture and trade. The same point is illustrated today by the two super-powers. Their superiority is most evident in the field of weaponry and other military preparations. But supporting and balancing these are other factors of a cohesive nature: the extent and compactness of their territories, prodigious natural resources, heroic pasts which feed their national identities, and deep-seated habits of political obedience whenever their territories are under threat. It would be as absurd to regard these sources of power as merely means or pre-conditions of military, and in particular of nuclear, predominance, as to ignore their indispensability for super-power status.

Nevertheless there are situations in which the two main aspects of power get out of balance and even work against each other. The internal cohesion of a great state, e.g. Manchu China, may become so seemingly complete and self-assured that new needs and means of compellent (or repellent) power are neglected, with disastrous results. Much more common is the opposite case in which a state, whose internal cohesiveness is questionable, becomes intoxicated with its temporary compellent superiority over its neighbours and rivals and launches out in military ventures which it cannot sustain. (Early eighteenth-century Sweden is the obvious European example.) But the present imbalance between cohesive and compellent power which threatens mankind is of a quite different kind, and on a quite different scale, from either of these examples. The present imbalance, although most strikingly exemplified in the nuclear rivalry and distrust of the super-powers is potentially a world-phenomenon. It lies in the grotesque disparity between the global destruction which any nuclear power, no matter how minor and irresponsible, can wreak or at least initiate by a single desperate act of would-be compellence, and the capacity to control or forestall such a disaster that is today possessed by any nation or alliance of nations.

This situation is the result, not simply of the recent gigantic advances in industrial and military technology, but of an implicit assumption on the part of all major powers during the later stages of the Europeanization or westernization of the world. The unspoken assumption of that venture was that, at every stage of it and particularly as it neared completion, *one* nation – perhaps France, perhaps Russia, perhaps Britain, perhaps Germany, perhaps America – would prove to be 'top nation', if not permanently at least for the foreseeable future. That nation would then dominate the world until, either through failure of its inward cohesiveness or through worldwide change in industrial and military technology, its supremacy was challenged. Thereupon the international struggle for world supremacy would be resumed by war and other means. But the incomparable destructiveness of nuclear weapons and the near-equality of our two super-powers give the lie to both these assumptions. While each super-power is militarily unassailable, neither can hope to win over the rest of the world to its ideology, without risking nuclear war or – an even more likely danger – without a gradual but fatal proliferation of nuclear weapons. There is no escape from this dilemma unless and until two steps are taken together: and taken together by the super-powers although in some sense they may have to be forced into taking them. The first is that they should agree to reduce their nuclear forces to equality but keep them at a level high enough to be patently unassailable by any third power. The second is that, in place of their present crazy over-kill capacities, the super-powers shall devise, direct and man *together* an intervention force capable of preventing any third power – be it national or piratical or terrorist or whatever – from threatening or practising nuclear blackmail in any part of the world. The first of these conditions provides the ultimate power behind the second: the second – the prospective experience of joint surveillance, and of constabulary and interventionist activity by the super-powers – provides the new and much needed motive for maintaining the first. Commanding and cohesive power would thus regain control over the run-away force of compellent power in the nuclear age. The first of these conditions is vaguely and hesitantly being recognized by the super-powers. But the second, without which the first has no real future, is something of a taboo subject. It appears to be unthinkable, mainly because almost no one dares to talk about it.

It has, however, been discussed by a number of eminent political theorists and publicists, in particular John Strachey, Richard Falk and Herman Kahn.[2] But none of these has set it out within an adequate doctrine of political power, or has envisaged the very special conditions under which alone, it seems to me, a 'nuclear diarchy' between America and Russia could come into being. I shall be discussing these conditions in my next chapter. But at this stage in my argument it will be useful to recall two initiatives, by politicians very much in the power-political tradition, which seem to me to foreshadow what I am proposing. Neither of these initiatives produced immediate results: but neither has lost its significance. The first is less well known than it deserves to be. A month after the dropping of the atom bomb on Hiroshima and Nagasaki, the American Secretary of State for War Henry Stimson wrote a memorandum to President Truman, in which he discussed the effect of the new explosive on American relations with the Soviet Union. He proposed a direct approach to Russia and also to Britain – in effect a continuation of World War II diplomacy – urging a tripartite plan for the control of the bomb for military purposes, while encouraging the development of atomic power for peaceful and humanitarian purposes. He explicitly rejected two ideas: first, that the 'atomic secret' should be used to wring concessions from the Russian leaders, and second that nuclear questions should not be placed in the hands of the newly formed United Nations Organization – a proposal which, Stimson felt, the Russians would reject out of hand. In the event his advice was neglected, and American policy fell between the two approaches which he condemned. There was an effort to work towards the internationalizing of nuclear matters: the Baruch Plan. This, however, left the control of atomic weapons in American hands pending a final and global agreement: a situation entirely unacceptable to Stalin who regarded it as a threat veiled in hypocrisy. Thereupon the Cold War set in, and after some thirty odd years the Soviet Union faced the United States as an equal in its capacity for nuclear over-kill.

I am not suggesting that Stimson's memorandum was a key to nuclear sanity which the Americans let slip and perhaps lost forever. Most informed people would agree that there was no real chance of a firm, constructive accord between the super-powers in the immediate post-war years. Neverthe less the views of a right-wing American Secretary of State for

War, expressed more than forty-five years ago, serve to remind us that the frozen duopoly and prolonged mutual distrust of the two super-powers was not the only conceivable answer to the problem of power in this nuclear age. The phrase 'a nuclear power' might have come to carry a very different meaning from that which we now attach to it. It might have meant a power which, thanks to its resources, geographical size and position, general military (including nuclear) strength, and inner self-confidence and cohesion, was in a position to commit itself, along with one or perhaps two other powers, to the task of containing and damping down any inter-state conflict which threatened to develop into nuclear war. More simply, 'a nuclear power' could have meant a power committed to and capable of maintaining nuclear peace, because of the intolerability of nuclear war. In the condition of the world at the end of World War II, only one power – America – was actually or immediately in a position to take up this role. Fifteen years later it had become plain that Britain was incapable of sustaining it, and that, in spite of the seeming paradox, Russia must do so, if there is ever to be an acceptable, that is a balanced and effective protection against nuclear disaster.

The second initiative which I want to recall is much better known: and because of the atmosphere of relief and near-euphoria which briefly surrounded it, it soon became suspect to politically sophisticated ears. It was President Kennedy's Commencement Address to the American University in Washington delivered on 10 June 1963, seven months after the resolution of the Cuba crisis, and five months before his assassination. It is not important who actually penned the speech: what matters is that an American President delivered it. Nor does it matter now that the immediate purpose of the speech was to give an emotional boost to the Kennedy administration's project of a comprehensive nuclear test ban – a project soon to be abandoned, because of Congressional opposition, and replaced by the partial test ban treaty, signed in Moscow in the following July. The very vagueness of the proposed *rapprochement* with the USSR could have acted as a challenge to new thinking about the change which super-power relations could begin to take. But this was not to be. Nevertheless the simple good sense of the speech's opening sentences, as well as its often-quoted conclusions, remain unaffected by its practical failure. 'Total war makes no sense in an age when great powers can maintain large and relatively invulnerable forces and refuse to surrender without resort to those forces. It makes no sense in an age when the deadly poisons produced by a nuclear exchange would be carried by wind and water and soil and seed to the four corners of the world and to generations yet unborn.' Then, after expressing the hope that the Soviet leaders would now alter their attitude, the President added the remarkable comment: 'I believe that we can help them to do this. But I also believe that we must examine our own attitude as individuals and as a Nation – for our attitude is as essential as theirs.' And having warned his fellow country-men 'not to see only distorted desperate views of the other side, not to see conflicts as inevitable, accommodation as impossible and communication as nothing more than an exchange of threats', he concluded: 'So let us not be blind to our differences – but let us also direct our attention to our common interests and the means by which those differences can be resolved. And if we cannot end now our differences, at least we can help make the world safe for diversity. For . . . our most basic common link is that we all inhabit this small planet. We all breathe the same air. We all cherish our children's future. And we are all mortal.' Whatever Kennedy's failings or superficialities as a politician, here he spoke with a unique authority. No other human being – not even Khrushchev – had had the experience of stepping so close to the brink of nuclear war.

What remains of compelling interest in this speech is that it comes so close to recognizing something that is today emerging into fuller light after the intervening twenty-five odd years of relative shadow. Almost from the outset of the

Cold War, and certainly from the death of Stalin onwards, the super-powers kept on surprising themselves – and each other – by their ability to settle down to useful discussion of minor differences between them. They feared and distrusted one another, yet they were aware, however dimly and unwillingly, of something of immense importance which they shared: their military, and more specifically after the 1950s their nuclear, invulnerability, always assuming that they were sane enough not to risk universal nuclear destruction. Granted this condition, each was invulnerable to the other and, *a fortiori*, to any lesser power. Unfortunately, after Kennedy's death and Khrushchev's removal, lack of political vision on either side prevented further exploration and constructive building upon this seemingly obvious truth. No one recognized, except in too abstract a way a few strategic analysts, that the basic 'rules of the game' of international relations had been transformed by the invention of nuclear weapons. Hitherto that game had been played on the assumption that, just as there always had been, so there always would be a tendency for political power to collect in a few centres – or sometimes in one centre – as a result of proven and accepted military superiority. Such concentrations of power might sometimes last for a long time, as in Chinese history or in southern Europe under the Romans, but, as a rule, lack of resources, and of information and communications, prevented them from lasting for long. Nevertheless, no sooner had one hegemony or empire collapsed under pressure from outside or under its own weight, than a new centre of power would appear as if to fill the gap. And always the main instrument and test of such dominant power would be superiority in war. But now the possession of nuclear weapons by the two super-powers, in approximately equal numbers and destructive capacity, has brought an end to this process. What, therefore, is left of the game of international relations? Are the two super-powers reduced to gazing glumly at each other from the security of their respective irreducible counter-strike capacities, while the rest of the world continues to play at war-games of minor significance?

As we saw in the concluding section of chapter 2, this last suggestion was unrealistic. It neglected the irresistible progress of technology, and hence the erosion of even the most seemingly perfect weapon-systems. It neglected the persistent effects of the ideological and economic rivalry between the super-powers. It neglected the dangers of the proliferation of nuclear weapons, even if on a small scale and in the most unreliable forms. And it neglected the important truth that, in all political life, the best safeguard against disastrous conflict is co-operation in some positive enterprise. These failures in political vision, however, point towards, even if they do not identify, what could have been done by the two super-powers in the light of the nuclear transformation of the international scene. What they have failed to see at all clearly – and perhaps this has been something which, to be seen clearly, must be seen slowly – is that the nuclear stalemate between them, taken in conjunction with danger posed by the general availability of nuclear weapons, presented them with an *opportunity* unparalleled in the history of mankind. The two super-powers are in a position in which they can probably impose a limited but biologically crucial form of peace, i.e., a nuclear peace upon the world as a whole. But the different ways in which this might be done, and the ways in which it quite certainly cannot be done, are among the as yet unlearnt lessons of the nuclear age: the topic of the next chapter.

Notes

1   Martin Wight's *Power Politics* was published in 1946, as one in a series entitled 'Forward-looking pamphlets', by the Royal Institute of International Affairs (London).

2   See, for instance, John Strachey (1962) *On the Prevention of War*, London: Macmillan; Richard Falk (1975) *A*

Study of World Futures, New York: Macmillan; Herman Kahn (1964) *Thinking about the Unthinkable*, New York: Greenwood Press.

6 The unlearnt lessons of the nuclear age

Let us begin from the narrower and simpler question: what have been the main lessons of the Cold War, which happily is no longer with us? The Cold War was a period of intense hostility between America and its allies and the Soviet Union and its allies: hostility which remained frozen, and did not burst forth into open war, largely because each side dreaded the prospect of another world war and, in particular, the irreversible destructiveness of the nuclear weapons which would be employed in it. But while appreciation of that destructiveness spread steadily, it hardly affected the initial rivalries which underlay the Cold War. The future of the world, it was assumed by both super-powers, would hinge on their competitive struggle for nuclear superiority: a struggle which was envisaged by each of them in somewhat different terms at its different stages, but which owed its constancy and direction to the spirit in which both parties had initially accepted it. For the Russians it meant, first, the breaking of the American nuclear monopoly; then the achieving of something close to nuclear parity; then successive clandestine bids for superiority – which, since 1988, they have wisely discarded. For the Americans it meant, first, a complacent assumption of nuclear superiority; then, after several nervous alerts, the determination to secure that superiority once and for all – an aim which has subsequently been modified by the belief that they always have had, and always will have, the capacity to regain and ensure it, whatever the future holds in store.

The history of this rivalry seems ordinary enough, until we remember the appalling possibilities, the appalling risks, that lay just under its surface. It then recalls a well-known nightmare situation. A number of adults are watching an excited band of children who have found a box of what they take to be toys but which (as the adults realize) are in fact dangerous explosive devices. Moreover it is clear that, as the children in their excitement delve deeper into the box, the larger and more dangerous are the devices which they pick out; and meanwhile the adults are paralysed with guilt and with the fear that, if they intervene, this will only make the children do wilder and more dangerous things. . . . There was another terrifying aspect of the Cold War. As it proceeded, and with every 'improvement' in nuclear weapons and their delivery systems, the more difficult it became to maintain a clear picture of what the whole business was in aid of or where it was tending. The latest secrets of nuclear gadgetry – whether jealously guarded or ruthlessly stolen – were felt to be the keys to final military superiority, while the figures of the 'over-kill' capacity of either super-power read like a production report from a factory staffed by imbeciles and directed by devils.

What, then, are the most important lessons of this terrifying chapter of human history, now mercifully ended and which mankind has had the good fortune to survive? It seems to me that there are only two. One is entirely negative, but has at last been recognized by the governments of the super-powers, if not as yet by the governments of other minor nuclear powers. The second lesson, although apparently positive in form and content, calls for so many qualifications and is so patently incomplete as it stands, that it can hardly be regarded as a great leap forward in the history of the nuclear age. Nevertheless, these lessons are worth considering with some care, since they make up the only intellectual capital which mankind has accumulated from the years of Cold War and therefore provide the springboard from which further constructive projects for war-avoidance must be launched. It hardly needs saying that these lessons do not even point to a *political agenda*, which must always be matched with circumstance and opportunity – a single daring political decision at the right moment being worth volumes of political programmatics. What my 'lessons' can do is to indicate the general directions in which initiative and effort must be made if mankind is to go forward into, and perhaps through, the nuclear age with some hope of survival.

The first of these lessons has already been mentioned. It is that the characteristic power-political response to the invention of nuclear weapons – that one or other of the super-powers must eventually show, once and for all, 'who is the master' – can no longer be hopefully pursued or sanely resumed. It is economically ruinous; it is politically puerile; it is morally abhorrent. It has to be stopped – that much is obvious. It has to be prevented from recurring – but how? Because there is nothing to be said in favour of its continuance, it is natural to infer that there is nothing to be learnt from the whole ghastly history of the Cold War and the nuclear arms-race which propelled it. Hence the natural and widespread desire simply to have done with it: a desire which motivates all projects for nuclear disarmament between East and West, whether unilateral or multilateral, whose hope is to establish a 'nuclear-free world'. But there is a fatal flaw and danger of disappointment in that hope. What reason is there to believe that nuclear disarmament by itself, even if it were carried to the ultimate limit, would produce a better and safer world-situation than the situation which obtained in Europe between the two world wars? And there is always the simpler danger that one of the super-powers, or perhaps some smaller but bitterly dissatisfied power, will resort to secret nuclear rearmament with a view to threatening nuclear blackmail if not outright war? These questions do not imply that the recent measures of nuclear disarmament, initiated by the Russians, are to be distrusted or despised. As an earnest rejection of Cold War assumptions they are sane and courageous, and they have already had a profound effect on popular opinion throughout the industrial world. But what constructive and permanent plans and moves should further them remains quite uncertain and, to all appearances, almost wholly unconsidered.

This brings us to the second main lesson of the Cold War. Its positive side calls for careful explanation, since at first blush it will seem repellent to many good people. And when that explanation is provided, its negative side – the conditions and qualifications which it involves and the issues which it does not even touch – leaves us with plenty of trouble on our hands. It is best introduced by the obvious but easily deceptive reflection that the Cold War has at least been kept cold and that there has been no open war between the super-powers. Why has this been so? No one can say exactly how big a part was played by the existence of nuclear weapons – whether in the early years of the American nuclear monopoly or in the later decades of near-equality between the super-powers – but it seems clear to me that it has been a big and probably indispensable one. (Be it noted that I am here speaking of the deterrent effect of the nuclear forces of the super-powers, not of, for example, those of Britain or France.) The ruthlessly competitive spirit in which each super-power developed its nuclear armoury; their shared delusion that the security of each depended at any given time upon the last increment of nuclear destructive power which it had been able to add to its armoury; and the crazy 'over-kill' capacity which each has eventually achieved, have blinded otherwise clear-sighted people to the one positive effect of the nuclear arms-race: namely, that it induced a saving degree of caution into the game of nerves, threats, bluffs and accusations in which the super-powers were engaged for most of forty years. Irrespective of the occasional crises and recurrent ups and downs of the Cold War, the dumb brute presence of the war-heads and missiles in their silos or under the oceans has acted as a kind of brake and warning-system on the moves and stratagems of the super-powers. Sanity has demanded that they do not go too far with their challenges and ripostes, since there stand the weapons – tangible evidence of irreversible destruction just round the corner if they take one step too far. This is what Professor McGeorge Bundy has aptly called the 'existential deterrent'[1]: the standing reminder of mankind's newly acquired and now ineradicable capacity for self-destruction embodied in the existence of nuclear weapons.

Of course this simple if painful lesson does not by itself justify the thirty-odd years of Cold War, or the present sizes and line-ups of the nuclear forces of the super-powers. The cost of the nuclear arms-race has been outrageously high, and is not to be computed only in economic terms: it will leave its traces, in prejudiced political judgements and undisclosed professional interests, for decades to come. Even now, when they have recognized that the function of mutual deterrence can be discharged by greatly reduced nuclear forces on either side, the super-powers have taken only one small step forward towards nuclear sanity and security. Left to themselves, in spite of their many differences, they could perhaps begin to move forward, step by step, towards a saner relationship. But the facts of the nuclear age will not leave them to themselves. Their present efforts to achieve mutual understanding do nothing to halt the spread of nuclear weapons which, especially in simplified, miniaturized forms, may prove more dangerous in the future than they were at the height of the Cold War. In addition to the three minor nuclear-powers (Britain, France and China) there are the half-dozen or so potential or would-be nuclear powers from whose amateurish hands oddments of nuclear weaponry and know-how may easily pass to irresponsible terrorist gangs or sub-states – by no means only in the Middle East. This is a danger which awaits us all in the next phase of the nuclear age, and with which the super-powers are as yet unprepared and unqualified to deal. They have stumbled almost simultaneously into a belated awareness of their great common interest. But they have been unable, as yet, to see what that common interest demands in terms of long-term policies or commitments.

What, then, is the first positive lesson which the super-powers must learn together if they – and the rest of us – are to emerge alive from the nuclear age? They could begin by asking themselves and each other how the unique advantage which each enjoys – that of military invulnerability from all quarters – could be used to give them both what they so patently lack: a corresponding measure of global respect and authority? No doubt Big Brothers are always likely to be envied, distrusted and even hated. But the kind of distrust which America and Russia severally succeeded in earning during the Cold War was of an unusually dangerous kind. Their adventures beyond their own borders have been pilloried with a bitter impotent cynicism, especially when – as has usually been the case – they went farcically and bloodily wrong. This is, of course, the characteristic reaction of the weak to the misfortunes of the strong. But, during the darkest phases of the Cold War, such cynicism was aggravated by a growing awareness of the appalling destructive power at the disposal of the super-powers and of their apparent indifference to the dangers to mankind as a whole which that power involved. To some extent that situation has been alleviated by the recent disarmament initiatives of the super-powers. But these have as yet been far from heartily welcomed by their allies. And the question remains: how can the super-powers develop policies of joint action which will quicken a sane hope for the human future?

Without going into useless fanciful specifics, I would suggest that there are three main lines of action along which progress can now be made towards nuclear sanity and security. (1) The super-powers, with the new prestige which their recent disarmament initiatives have brought them, are now in a strong position to urge the three minor nuclear powers to reduce their nuclear forces in corresponding fashion, even if this betokens their early disappearance from the strategic scene. Indeed on this issue the super-powers might well succeed in appealing directly to the peoples of the minor nuclear powers over the heads of their unwilling governments. (2) They should also enlist the aid of the minor nuclear and of other advanced industrial powers in a much more effective ban on the spread of nuclear materials and know-how which are of potential military significance. (3) And they should break new ground by seeking general support – economic and technical and financial – for a programme, under joint American–Russian direction, of worldwide surveillance and, where necessary, of military interference to nip in the bud any signs of nuclear adventurism or threats of nuclear war.

This last step will no doubt seem unthinkable to many people – chiefly because it has almost never been seriously thought about. And people have not thought about it seriously because this would mean moving into a new chapter of human thought and action. It would mean (or at least it would threaten) the end of that epoch in which it has seemed inevitable that governments should employ the strongest (i.e., the most destructive) weapons that are available to them in order to advance or secure what seem to be their vital interests. But the supreme lesson of the nuclear age (into whose second phase we are all now stepping) is that the most urgent interest of all governments is human survival (especially that of their own peoples), and that for this reason the strongest instruments of war will have to be given a radically altered role in human life. Nuclear weapons are bound to go on existing, because they cannot be uninvented, but it is possible that they should exist only in forms which are inherently controlling and controlled. Thus, I would argue, the super-powers should retain their nuclear forces, greatly reduced but approximately equal in size and strength, sufficient to ensure their invulnerability whether from each other or from any other quarter. In addition to these basic negative functions, their nuclear forces would serve a more positive purpose. Somewhat like the gold that is said to exist unused but never forgotten in the cellars of Fort Knox, they could act as a constant reminder, from this time onward, of mankind's now ineradicable capacity for self-destruction. This is something which, so far as can be foreseen, it will never be safe for any section of mankind to forget or neglect. And that is why it is imperative that the (greatly reduced) nuclear forces of the super-powers should be kept not only in *being* but, so to speak, on constant and open *exhibition*: powerless against each other by virtue of their equality, unchallengeable from any other quarter, and portentous as a warning of irremediable disaster if ever they were unleashed. Nuclear weapons, thus confined to and maintained by the two super-powers, would be a permanent bulwark against any slide into nuclear piracy or adventurism in any part of the world.

It would be unrealistic, however, to hope that the follies and frustrations of mankind can ever be held in check by warnings and reminders alone. Hence the need for the project, mentioned above, of a joint super-power surveillance and intervention force, ready for action at the first sign or threat of nuclear blackmail or war. But how could such a force or agency be initiated, organized, staffed and directed? How could it succeed in being at once a combined undertaking, yet capable of immediate effective military action? How could it escape the danger of internal frictions and divisions? How could one guarantee that its intelligence findings reached the appropriate ministries of both super-powers? And by what main tactical means would it act? By corralling or quarantining or disabling or forcibly destroying any action which looked like sparking off a nuclear war? And within whose judgement would that act of interpretation and decision lie? To speak more concretely, are we here thinking in terms of super-Entebbean raids, or perhaps of the need and the authority to move whole populations – by millions if necessary – in case the suppression of some act of nuclear piracy required the violent destruction of the pirate's nuclear

apparatus? These are questions for which no one unac-
quainted with the contemporary war plans, war machines and
war exercises, can suggest even the outlines of a practicable
answer. But it seems to me more than likely that, given free
access to the secret files of the Pentagon and the Kremlin, an
enterprising team of military men, engineers, scientists and
international lawyers could quickly come up with some useful
suggestions. (I have heard that war plans for the most
eccentrically conceived contingencies exist in certain War
Offices.) This is not to belittle the difficulties which would
evidently beset the sort of agency that I have in mind. It
might well be open to abuses: it might sometimes involve
disasters. But it has attractions and assets which far outweigh
these dangers. It would amount to the first striking and
unmistakable move *against* the ever-rising tide of destructiveness that is inherent in the generally accepted practice and
justifications of war. As such it might well receive a degree of
worldwide support unparalleled in previous history. Add to
this that the sharp ideological differences between the super-
powers would ensure that they fulfil their tasks of surveillance and intervention in a spirit, not only of mutual support,
but of mutually watchful criticism, thus ensuring that they do
not act beyond the limits of their special remit. At the same
time, the proposed 'teams' would be animated by the sense
of engaging in an altogether novel exercise of power: every
member of them being aware that it is only in combination
with his former foes and rivals that he can secure the survival
of his own people – and incidentally that of the other peoples
of the world.

What I am here suggesting is a somewhat more concrete
and tangible version of the conclusion which I formulated at
the end of chapter 2, namely that the invention of nuclear
weapons has faced men with the choice between a revolution
in their moral *and* political *and* strategic thinking or their
own self-destruction, i.e. that they must become war-
containing or at least nuclear-war-diverting animals, or else
perish. That conclusion was arrived at through a critique of

the thesis that Mutually Assured Destructive Capability provided, however paradoxically, an escape-route from the nuclear problem. What this thesis neglected, most obviously, was the kind of morally and politically *innovative* effort that wouldd be required if this paradoxical opportunity were to be exploited. But the doctrine of MADC neglected something else: namely that the most effective (because most destructive) military means which men find in their hands have not come there, so to speak, out of the blue. Nuclear weapons would not be weapons of war, if they did not serve to express the assumption that superior weaponry will always win for men all or most of what they want from their enemies and neighbours. It is the age-old cult of superiority in war-materials that has somehow to be diverted or turned back on its tracks now that the ultimately superior weapon has proved itself to be so destructive as to be unusable. And it is for this reason that the bewildering paradox 'the only possible use of nuclear weapons is to ensure that they are never actually used' needs to be presented in relatively concrete and tangible terms, so that it can counter and undercut the age-old nostrum 'If you want peace, prepare for war'. It must be brought home to the great mass of mankind that, since the game of war in its ultimate nuclear forms has become biologically intolerable, its traditional rules and its ultimate tools must also be re-fashioned and even, in some respects, put into reverse.

The success of the project now under discussion must depend very largely on how it is politically presented. And on this score there are a number of hopeful considerations which political publicists, both in the West and the East, are liable to neglect. Once the idea of a joint Russian–American nuclear-war prevention agency was floated, and still more once it was known to have taken shape, public response to it, not only in Russia and America but in a great many other countries, would almost certainly be positive. The simplest men and women in the world, along with the most politically sophisticated, would be at one in recognizing that *at last* something serious was being done to save their children from horrific extinction. To pursue this line of thought only a little way: once a number of teams of highly specialized troops and technicians, drawn in equal number from both super-powers, were known to be at work in joint surveillance duties and in training for joint intervention whenever necessary, their very existence would act as a brake on any resurgence of military rivalry between the super-powers. In this respect, the combined teams would resurrect the functions which hostages originally discharged in the ancient world: viz. that of persons left behind with an enemy as a pledge for the fulfilment of a treaty. While expressly selected and trained to forestall the danger of nuclear war, the teams would also serve to keep the peoples and governments of the super-powers in mind of the radically changed meaning of power in the world of today. Secure against any head-on nuclear attack – from each other or from any third party – by virtue of their retained, although greatly reduced, nuclear forces, and united in their function of forestalling or suppressing any new threats of future nuclear adventurism, the super-powers could at last claim to be acting, in this one crucial field, as world powers in a world cause.

Of course it seems paradoxical to argue that, in a world threatened with nuclear destruction, the only means of salvation lies with the two powers which are fully equipped to realize this threat. But once the required imaginative leap is made, the very idea of the two super-powers acting together on the one issue of preventing nuclear war promises a new chapter in human history. War between highly industrialized countries having become intolerable, the military skills and capacities of the two super-powers can have no rational role other than that of preventing it in its most terrible and irreversible form. For what are the alternatives? On the one side, a nuclear monopoly, which history has rendered impossible and which in any case would mean a global tyranny. On the other side, a nuclear anarchy which would be a recipe for general destruction. Any more complex organization of nuclear powers – say a triarchy – would be open to the danger of a two-to-one split among the partners. As against these possibilities, a nuclear diarchy, especially between powers of strikingly different economic and political traditions, has the merit of an almost naked simplicity. Both parties would be aware of the danger-spots in their relationship. Both would know that they were engaged in a historic, do-or-die venture, from which no retreat is possible: that they must create together a novel and highly specialized form of power to ensure human survival.

Thus far I have been arguing, in defence and clarification of the idea of a nuclear diarchy, as though, because its operation must lie with the super-powers, it follows that the initial demand for it and the initial steps towards it must also come from them. But, although at the moment this seems the most likely course of events, it is not the only one to be considered. The boot may well be on the other foot. The initiative, the canvassing, the pressures for a nuclear diarchy may come from a group of minor powers who would have the task of selling the idea to the super-powers. Such an approach may seem strange to us but it was quite familiar to the peoples of antiquity. The literatures of the Hebrews and the ancient Greeks contain moving accounts of mass-supplications, made by tribes or cities or nations, to some ruler who (it was hoped) would save them from afflictions which they could not master by themselves. In our world such an approach – couched in UN officialese – would be less dramatic, but the need which it expresses would be no less appealing. And the super-powers, whose leaders claim to represent the human future, would find it almost impossible to ignore. There is, however, one quarter from which resistance to such an initiative must be expected: those governments and peoples that derive both pride and comfort from their status as nuclear powers, no matter how minor, how costly and imperfectly independent their nuclear forces may be. Is it conceivable that the peoples of Britain and

France would be content to live and conduct their external relations under the protection of a super-power nuclear diarchy of the kind I am proposing? Before this could possibly happen, a good deal of basic political re-education would be needed, particularly in Britain. People of all parties, classes and age-groups must become accustomed to asking – and to listening to alternative answers to – the question: in what circumstances and from what motives is it likely, or even conceivable, that the Soviet Union would choose to attack, occupy, despoil or totally destroy the liberties and wealth of Great Britain? Britain's most obvious assets are its industrial and intellectual expertise and its highly developed international trade connections, which are not the kinds of thing that could be transplanted easily to eastern Europe; while its main disadvantages to any prospective conqueror and enslaver are the character and outlook of its people – on the surface indolent, incurious and over-confident, but capable, under pressure, of unusual stubborn-ness, resistance and flare. As a (highly hypothetical) choice for an ambitious Russian Commissar, it is hard to think of a less desirable foreign assignment than that of an 'occupied' Britain – until one thinks of an occupied France or Switzerland or Spain.

Moreover, Britain *by itself* poses no obvious threat – military or political or economic – to Soviet Russia; a wholesome combination of distance and difference has in the past ensured generally good relations between the two peoples, one situated on the western, one on the eastern, edge of Europe. The only serious ground for a Russian attack on Britain that I can think of, would be that the Soviet military leaders would come to regard Britain as too dangerous an advance base for an American attack on their territories, and would therefore decide to 'take it out', in order to pre-empt a general nuclear war. But this, evidently, would not be an attack on Britain as such, or a threat of a blow which Britain's nuclear forces could prevent by the threat of nuclear response. It would be the first blow in a much larger game; that hideously misconceived battle for global supremacy between the super-powers which would be the end of human civilization. As we have seen, however, the super-powers have always shown great caution in the face of this horrific possibility. Their respective 'existential deterrents' have kept them sane. And in this operation of existential deterrence, Britain's relatively small nuclear forces have played no part whatsoever. Or, to speak more plainly, Britain's contribution to nuclear peace has, throughout the years of the Cold War, been simply *nil*. This is not a fault that can be attributed to any particular British administration. But it is essential that it should be recognized, so that Britain can begin to make a genuine if ostensibly minor contribution to the maintenance of peace in the nuclear age.

By what stages, and subject to what guarantees, Britain could transform its role, from that of a minor appendage to the West–East nuclear rivalry to that of an important under-worker – one might almost say midwife – in the cause of nuclear sanity, is the question which should be at the heart of British politics today. To be sure, the future of the British nuclear deterrent has played a major part in recent British general elections, but it has done so in an absurdly misleading way. The British electorate has, in effect, been invited to choose between two equally inane alternatives: either to continue playing a very minor but hugely self-deceiving part in the West–East nuclear rivalry, or simply to step out of the whole business with a sense of 'what a good person am I'. Neither of these alternatives contributes in any positive way toward the solution of the nuclear problem: each is therefore a kind of insult to a democratic electorate. Each reflects those habits of basic non-thinking about war against which this book is directed, and, more particularly, each shies away from admitting that a defence policy, originally chosen for good enough reasons, can very soon prove to be discharging no positive function whatsoever. A glance back at the unhappy history of the British nuclear deterrent, and a few comparisons between its fate and those of the French and Chinese deterrent forces, will help to drive home this conclusion.

The history of the British nuclear deterrent began admirably, but quickly passed into disappointment, frustration and self-deception. The original decision 'to construct a super bomb based on a nuclear chain reaction in uranium' was taken, in the early months of World War II, for a reason that was perhaps unique in the history of war: not to achieve victory by means of a new and irresistible weapon, but to forestall the use of such a weapon by the Nazi government of Germany. In the circumstances of war no responsible person could have complained of this decision and its purpose was brilliantly assured when, a few years later, a British-Norwegian commando destroyed the heavy-water plants in Norway, from which the Nazis had planned to develop their own nuclear weapons. The next step, at once generous and realistic, was to transfer the initial British experiments to America, partly for security reasons, but chiefly because in this way far more resources – material, financial and intellectual – could be channelled into the project under American leadership. This step was taken on the understanding that Anglo-American co-operation in the field of nuclear weapons would continue into the years of peace. But when the Truman administration reneged on this agreement in 1946, the British post-war Labour government was put into a very difficult position. To Attlee and his senior Labour Party colleagues it seemed as natural as it would have done to Winston Churchill and his Conservative colleagues, that Britain, as one of the three main victorious powers, should continue to have a say in the development and control of nuclear weapons. And as much out of pique against the Americans as out of fear and distrust of the Russians, Attlee and his colleagues decided, in spite of Britain's crippled material and financial condition, to go it alone. It is difficult not to sympathize, and indeed not to commend their decision, although pique is a dangerous motive in politics.

especially when it leads to a plunge into the unknown. Later on, in the 1950s, Aneurin Bevan was to defend the retention of the British bomb on the grounds of national prestige. Without it, he argued, any future Labour Foreign Secretary would have to go 'naked into the conference chambers', and would be unable to urge moderation on the (by then) bitterly hostile and mistrustful super-powers. But in this commendable hope and presumption Bevan was wrong. In all serious discussions of nuclear weapons save one – that which, thanks to Harold Macmillan's efforts, produced the partial Test Ban Treaty of 1964 – Britain has been virtually ignored by the two great nuclear antagonists. The Russians have regarded us as a second-rate satellite or advance base of America, and the Americans have tended to regard our nuclear forces as a tiresome complication in whatever disarmament negotiations were on hand. This last point was made woundingly explicit when, in the early 1960s, the Americans cancelled successively the production of their Blue Streak and of their Skybolt missiles which the British government had hoped to buy: and this wound was not completely healed by the relatively generous but still somewhat ambiguous terms on which the Polaris missile system was eventually purchased as the main vehicle of Britain's nominally independent deterrent. Even the purchase of the Trident system by the Thatcher government is dogged by the suspicion that, since its re-fitting and updating will require American facilities, its use – always supposing that this could ever be seriously contemplated – would still be subject to American control.

Considered retrospectively and as a whole, therefore, Britain's determination to become an independent nuclear power has been flawed by a confusion of two natural but incompatible aims: to maintain the independence characteristic of a great power while at the same time relying on the support and protection of the greatest of the super-powers. This confusion has been the main cause of British humiliations, delusions and even deliberate self-deceptions on the score of nuclear weapons. The official reasons for the necessity of a British nuclear deterrent (which governments wisely refer to as seldom as possible) make painfully implausible, and indeed intellectually blush-making, reading today. There are three of them. First, it is claimed that the British nuclear forces make a direct, if admittedly minor, contribution to the general defence of the West. Secondly and more specifically, the British deterrent is said to add an important element of uncertainty to any situation for which Russian planners have to make their calculations, since they can never be sure how or where or with what cohesion American and British nuclear forces would respond to this or that move or threat on their part. Thirdly, should the Russians ever threaten Britain on an issue or in an area over which the Americans refused to intervene, the British nuclear deterrent, although relatively small, is powerful enough to make the Russians think twice about what they are doing. The objection to the first of these excuses for the British deterrent is that it is superfluous: the objection to the second is that, at a time when the super-powers are engaged in confidence-building measures, it is mischievous: the objection to the third is that, if it were seriously enacted or even threatened, it could well prove to be suicidal. Moreover, as has often been pointed out, there has been no serious international issue of the last thirty odd years, to whose resolution Britain's nuclear capability has contributed in any way.

The majority of the British public is unwilling to recognize these facts because to do so seems to be an acceptance of Britain's 'inferiority'. But there is nothing shameful in recognizing that in respect of its nuclear capability Britain is now only a minor power. Moreover it cannot be emphasized too often that this apparent 'inferiority' is a result as much of geography as of relative economic and military weakness. Britain (and the same holds for all West European nations) is a sitting target for a nuclear first-strike in a way that Russia and America (and for that matter Canada, China and Brazil) are not. Not that there is much to choose between sudden extinction and a long drawn out disintegration as a result of nuclear war. But, considered in terms of nuclear blackmail, the threat of immediate extinction has a peculiar dis-attraction of its own. And for this reason among others it is high time that the British people abandoned the illusion that their nuclear pretensions are the main thing that still keeps Britain great. These remarks may sound unpleasantly dismissive. But they are necessary, because the consequences to which Britain's attachment to her nuclear deterrent may lead could well be disastrous. As we have seen, Britain's part in the early stages of the nuclear age was a most creditable one. But her latter-day situation – as a nuclear power without a positive function – is of importance mainly as an object lesson to other minor powers with an ambition for nuclear status. More than this, however, Britain is capable of endangering super-power relations by playing on the deep-seated suspicions and anxieties of American minds. There are indeed no limits to which governments of a declining power may not be tempted to go to preserve what they consider to be their rightful international status: and there is a ruthless side to traditional British diplomacy which tends to confuse wrecking tactics with political realism. Herein lie the dangers which it would be dangerous to condone or gloss over, and which reappear – although in very different nationalist trappings – in the history of the French nuclear deterrent.

When General de Gaulle returned to power in France in 1958, his aims – to restore France to a condition of national efficiency, self-respect and world-repute – were continuous with those which he had embodied so remarkably in 1940. The means available to him were of course very different, and the main planks of his 1958 political programme were radical constitutional reform, disengagement from Algeria and France's colonial empire, and reconciliation with Germany with a view to a joint leadership of Europe. To these, all of which showed the stamp of statesmanship, he added a fourth: the creation of a French nuclear striking force, in complete independence of America and Britain. This was the weakest part in de Gaulle's platform: and the element of anti-British, anti-American pique in its motivation strangely echoed the pique which had inspired Britain's decision to 'go nuclear' twelve years earlier. De Gaulle's determination that his *force de frappe* should be an entirely French production put an immense financial burden on his country; and, in the event, his nuclear force had to be so restricted that it could promise no protection to France's European allies. It was presented as simply a weapon of last resort, for the protection of the sacred soil of France.

De Gaulle had been among the first to perceive that the only possible uses of nuclear weapons were political. But what results did this pithy insight have in practice? De Gaulle failed to see how drastically the areas and directions of political influence and action had been altered by the discovery of nuclear weapons. He saw clearly some of the changes which France's situation demanded, but he did not appreciate the changing background over and against which these changes had to be contrived. What important effects can in truth be attributed to his *force de frappe*? Has it affected the calculations and conduct of the super-powers? Has it strengthened France's global repute – except in the form of bitter resentment against her nuclear tests in the South Pacific? The answer is 'No' or 'Very little', every time. And when we come to France's internal well-being, the results are far from reassuring. The requirements of the *force de frappe* have played a major part in committing France to a dependence upon nuclear fuels for its industrial renewal, at what heavy economic and environmental costs it is still impossible to decide. Are we to say, then, that France's achievement of nuclear-weapons status was a sheer mistake, an absurd Gaullist gesture, attributable to *folie de grandeur*?

By no means. As in the case of the British nuclear deterrent, no one could possibly have foreseen how the logic of nuclear rivalry would work its way out in the second half of our century. If France's nuclear ambitions, like Britain's, have proved to be mistaken, this does not mean that they are something to be ashamed of – and worse, something to be cloaked or lied about, or defended by ever less plausible arguments. What matters now is the general lesson that can be drawn from France's mistake, which is clearer than that of Britain because of the latter's ambiguous dependence upon American aid and agreement. This lesson is of particular importance to any rising or reviving power which may in future be tempted to prove its status through the possession of a minor nuclear force. Not only should any such power ask itself, very seriously, what specific functions its nuclear force could fulfil: it should recognize in advance, in the light of the French experience, that it can have no positive function, only at best a certain nuisance value, in a world in which the primary task of international politics is to prevent any future war from escalating to the nuclear level: a task which demands decisive and untrammelled action such as can be expected, in the foreseeable future, only from America and Russia working together.

Finally, a word about the much more mysterious role of the Chinese nuclear deterrent. Notoriously, because of its geographical position, its vast size and population, its notable resources and economic backwardness, as well as its peculiar history and culture, China seems to most westerners to be a world on its own. But nuclear military capacity, like death, is a great leveller, and there are at least three comparisons with the cases of Britain and France which can help us to think, sanely and warily, about the Chinese nuclear deterrent. First, it seems most unlikely that any hostile power will ever again invade China, with a view to effecting its permanent conquest: as a means of military defence or deterrence, therefore, China is unlikely to expand its nuclear forces very greatly or rapidly. Secondly, it is hard to see how China's nuclear status can greatly add to her influence with those nations and governments of the Third World which she has aspired to lead and support against the domination of the

West. Thirdly, if we consider the greatest question that affects China's future – which power or powers will eventually determine the economic development of the Pacific basin – it again seems unlikely that China's small nuclear forces will prove to be relevant. There is not much that a few nuclear bombs can do to regulate the growth of populations or of capital investment. This does not mean, however, that China would easily submit to the kind of nuclear diarchy, between America and Russia, which I have advocated. But here we reach difficulties on which it is as yet impossible even to speculate. Of all the imponderable issues of the nuclear age those arising from China are perhaps the gravest and may turn out to be the most surprising.

The lessons which, if I am right, have still to be learnt if mankind is to survive the nuclear age, stand out by virtue of their simple urgency. But there is one respect in which they show an affinity to a cluster of other lessons which mankind seems more ready to recognize, but which in the end may prove equally difficult and hardly less important. These lessons concern such closely inter-related issues as the preservation of the global environment, the resolution of the so-called North–South divide, control of world health and of world population, as well as a curtailment of the current free-for-all global market in conventional arms. What all these tasks have in common with the prevention of nuclear war is that they demand much more effective global controls than have ever been attempted before, which in turn will require much greater international skills and a much higher level of international awareness than mankind has so far achieved. In particular they demand controls which must be administered with great sensitivity to national and regional differences – and values and touchinesses – if they are to be tolerated. Hence the politics of the future, which will be centred on international politics, will have to follow very different guidelines and will demand notably different qualities from those of traditional national politics. But among mankind's different arduous tasks, the prevention of war in its most developed forms, nuclear or post-nuclear war, seems destined to play the part of a pilot study. If the nations of the world can agree to support a nuclear diarchy between west and east to preserve themselves from nuclear destruction, they will be encouraged to work out equally effective means of preserving, within necessary limitations, their fruitful but inevitably frictional diversity.

Note

1   See McGeorge Bundy (1984) 'The unimpressive record of atomic diplomacy', in *The Choice: Nuclear Weapons versus Security*, London, Chatto and Windus.

7 War Studies, Peace Studies and Survival Studies

For what kind of reader is this book intended? Like any other serious book it has been written partly for my own satisfaction: to pull together certain ideas, to work out certain arguments, to explore certain possible lines of political action. Naturally a writer hopes that his or her own interests will coincide, at least partly, with those of his readers, so that they will respond positively to the leads. Such coincidence is most likely to be complete when a book's appeal is mainly logical or mainly aesthetic. Yet there are books whose effect is to be measured by the response of their readers, even when that response varies from critical doubt to regretful disagreement. The function of such books is to make people sit up and think, to start worrying or to worry to somewhat better purpose. Where, then, do I look for readers who will repond to this book's appeal?

My answer is rather complicated. There is a small professional audience which I would like my book to reach and influence. But there is also a far larger, far from professionally identifiable audience – men and women of widely differing interests, classes and age-groups, whom I would like my book to reach, but chiefly by putting them in touch with the smaller professional group which I mentioned first. From neither group do I look for complete agreement: my hope is, rather, that by helping to bring them into

105

contact, my book will also help to make them together into a significant intellectual force.

Who then, first, are the selected few? Their central core consists of those teachers and researchers who are engaged in two as yet sadly underdeveloped branches of higher education in this country and elsewhere: War Studies and Peace Studies. But pressing upon and overlapping this central core is a wider fringe of academic teachers, researchers, students and administrators who would be more than happy to see War Studies and Peace Studies playing a larger part in higher education. Here, then, is the small professional audience which I would like my book to reach. What of the second, wider, less easily identifiable audience?

This, as I have said, is not confined to any one professional group or indeed to any one intellectual type of person. Not to professional politicians or political commentators and analysts, nor even to those who are vaguely described as 'intellectuals'. Naturally, the wider readership which I hope for consists of persons of fairly quick and vigorous intelligence, with a living interest in the human past and a deeply felt concern for the human future, and with a compelling urge to focus that concern more effectively. But, for the rest, he or she is no more likely to be found in the ranks of scientists or of medicals, of civil servants or of clergymen, of artists or of social workers than in any other walk of life. This person is the proverbial 'man in the street', to be found anywhere and everywhere. He is no rarity: but, being scattered, he is likely to feel isolated. He may be convinced that there are millions who feel as mystified and horrified as he does by the fact that through recent development of warfare man has become mankind's worst enemy, and that, in spite of the present easement in the rivalry of the super-powers, every nation in the world today is liable to be threatened, if not immediately snuffed out, by a renewed outburst of nuclear hysteria. But he may feel equally unhappy with popular explanations and pro-posed remedies for this state of affairs. None of them, he senses, goes deep enough, or sees – or even looks – widely enough. None helps him to see a road along which he, his children and his children's children can advance with hope. In short he is longing for enlightened guidance, but has no idea where to look for it.

In this situation it is only natural to ask: how could these two groups be brought closer together? One answer to this might be: through a book which tries to bring into a sharper intellectual focus the vague but powerful anxieties of my 'man in the street' and to provide a point of growth and of properly popular appeal to our somewhat narrowly orien-tated schools of War Studies and Peace Studies. This, very roughly, is what the present book has tried to do. It remains to discuss, however – but only in the most general terms – whether its aim is feasible and deserves to be taken seriously. And this, I think, can best be done by putting two somewhat awkward, not to say, contentious questions. Can anyone reasonably maintain that, as currently taught – and indeed well taught – in our universities, either War Studies or Peace Studies or some amalgam of both could do anything to lighten the anxieties of my 'man in the street', conscious as he is of his species' seemingly fatal propensity for war? To this, I am afraid, the answer is No. Yet this leaves open the possibility that these recently developed branches of study might be re-orientated to fulfil a much larger educational task than has so far been assigned to them. Secondly, can we reasonably expect that our universities and polytechnics – and their directors and political masters – would ever countenance and encourage a larger extension of either War Studies or Peace Studies in their curricula? Again, the answer seems to be No – unless the proposed extension formed part of a more general revision and indeed regeneration of higher education in Britain. Later in this chapter I shall suggest some broad educational arguments for such a revision and regeneration. But before doing this, I must first show why, as at present taught, War Studies and Peace Studies are able to do so little to meet the needs of a larger waiting public.

War Studies and Peace Studies – the example of Britain

There are departments of War Studies and departments or schools of Peace Studies in only a few British universities, and these are relatively small and cannot be said to play a large part in higher education in Britain today. This is not to say that their teaching and research are not of a high quality. On the contrary, the quality is remarkably high. My complaint is that these departments have not been allowed to develop far enough, and that they have been able to supply only somewhat marginal courses to students with markedly specialized interests. Moreover they appear to offer very little assistance or support to one another.

This last point may, at first blush, seem natural enough. Indeed the juxtaposition of the titles 'War Studies' and 'Peace Studies' might well look odd to my 'man in the street'. From which – if either – would he hope to learn most, or to obtain most guidance as he faces the anomalies and paradoxes of the nuclear age? Does he really want to know more about wars – in different times and places, including our own century? Or does he really want to know more, in detail, about the different projects for containing or preventing war which have been advanced during these past two hundred-odd years? The main thesis of this book is that what we *all* need – the most learned and the least informed among us – is the capacity to think more clearly and confidently about war as an *ever* expanding dimension of human life. And while close study of particular wars or particular developments of warfare, or of recent endeavours in the field of war-prevention, may possibly assist us in this endeavour, they can do so only indirectly and *per accidens*. It is not the job of either War Studies or Peace Studies to help the 'man in the street' to realize *what war is* or to render it more intelligible and therefore more subject to rational control; and if we want to understand why this is so, we must consider the special conditions under which each of these studies has developed, the difficulties which each has had to face.

War Studies, as currently taught in a handful of universities and one polytechnic in Britain, naturally touch on important questions of law, economy, diplomacy, communications, public health etc.; but primarily they are a specialized outgrowth of historical study. Now historical study, in Britain as elsewhere, has been subject to different ideological influences and colourings during the last two centuries. But in the main, and mainly for very good reasons, War Studies have followed that central conservative historical tradition which concentrates upon uncovering 'what actually happened', in this, that or the other particular war or phase or field of warfare. And the main reason for this is that the facts of war – always complicated, confused, multi-layered and presented from different stand-points – are so liable to be disturbed by political interests or romanticized in national mythologies or to be obliterated in the sheer welter of war itself. This explains why War Studies, although essentially a special form of historical study, are a peculiarly narrow and constricted form of it. Detailed study of the means and methods of some particular war – say the Boer War or World War I – is not likely to add to that broad understanding of human life and action which is commonly and rightly expected from historical study. It is therefore unlikely to deepen our grasp of war's general role in history or of that inherently cumulative character which I have ascribed to war in earlier chapters of this book. In saying this I am not disparaging or even criticizing War Studies as currently taught. Those who teach and practise them do not claim to be philosophers or prophets of war or evangelists of war-prevention. But to acknowledge this is to explain why, as currently taught, they provide so little enlightenment or guidance to the man in the street, who is bewildered by the paradoxes of the nuclear age.

If War Studies fall short in this respect, do courses of Peace Studies do any better? My regretful conclusion is that they too fall short, although in a quite different way and from quite other causes. Pioneers of Peace Studies – and I have here chiefly in mind those of the admirable Bradford University School – have felt strongly the need to prove that peace is a proper subject of university study, and that their courses come up to required academic standards. Because of this they have chosen to present peace as an 'area study' in which methods and materials, already tested in other broader disciplines, notably sociology and political science, are applied to the questions of peace-making in a war-torn or war-threatened world. This is an attractive idea which may well produce notable results. But as an overall guiding policy, it has two marked weaknesses. It assumes that the problem of war in the nuclear age is simply a special case – admittedly a specially grave case – of the general problem of conflict-resolution, and it suggests that if only the techniques which have been devised for loosening up less dangerous conflicts could be sharpened and strengthened, we would well be on the way to freeing mankind from its nightmare fears of further and this time final global war. But peace-making in our time is not a new unexplored field lying open to theoretical and experimental exploration and control. It is a field of confused assumptions and beliefs, of whose worst consequences mankind has suddenly but still reluctantly become aware. It is the unique hugeness and awfulness of the prospect of nuclear war which now compels men's efforts to acquire a new self-knowledge and a radical re-direction of their international endeavours.

But there is a second and more specifically academic objection to the Bradford School's choice of 'tutelary' disciplines for the development of Peace Studies. Sociology and political science are, both of them, very wide-ranging disciplines, and quite clearly only a selection of their topics – in particular those concerned with conflict – would be relevant to Peace Studies. But there is one important characteristic which both these disciplines, in all their diverse developments, have in common. They are, both of them, manifestly *intra*-societal rather than *inter*-societal enquiries. Both concentrate upon political developments, tensions and conflicts within societies rather than upon those which occur between them. With only a few exceptions, neither has been greatly concerned with the ways in which wars between nations have distorted or stunted their internal developments. Neither to my knowledge has even registered astonishment at the extraordinary trust which almost all nations have placed in war as the instrument *par excellence* in international politics, in view of its appalling bluntness and the width of unforeseen and undesired results which it always brings in its train. It is not, therefore, surprising that during the present century the new discipline of International Relations should have arisen to fill this gap in the political and social sciences. But despite the excellent scholarly work that has been done in this field, it has as yet produced no results – no idea, no thesis, no warning – which could reinvigorate by widening the pursuit of either War Studies or Peace Studies.

These critical remarks point towards a fairly obvious conclusion: War Studies and Peace Studies need to be brought closer together, although there can be no simple amalgamation of them. What seems to me possible, however, as well as highly desirable, is that they should be considered as two main panels for a new design of 'survival studies' within higher education. The peculiarity of such studies would be the clear recognition that they are motivated by a deeply practical aim to defend, conserve and adapt civilized human values, most immediately from destruction in a nuclear or post-nuclear war. The conceptual re-vision of war which this book offers is designed to assist War Studies and Peace Studies to move towards each other in this urgently needed way. How far the idea of survival studies might be expanded – for instance to cover problems of a biological and environmental kind – I cannot here even begin to discuss.

But even from the more limited standpoint of this book, it is important to make clear how educationally ambitious and disturbing the project of survival studies will have to be if it is to fulfil the function that I assign to it.

In the first place it seems to me imperative that these studies shall have a compulsory but flexible place in all courses of higher education. No doubt different approaches, centred on the different main 'panels' of survival studies, could be devised to suit the interests and capacities of different types of student – mathematicians and experimentalists, historians and social scientists, lawyers and medicals, for example. The basic excuse for such compulsion – at first sight so offensive to the university spirit – is simple. The sciences and the humanities alike presuppose the continuity of civilized human living. The educationally most privileged members of any civilized community have therefore a special obligation to think continually, and to train others to think continually, about this basic condition of the privileges which they enjoy. In this connection, it is worth repeating Cardinal Newman's claim that the most important thing in university life is what students learn from one another. Or, in other words, the most important university subjects are those which most students discuss most eagerly together. At different periods in the past, different subjects have held this privileged position. In the Middle Ages theology and logic vied for it; at the Renaissance classical literature and mathematics vied for it: in the great age of Enlightenment the idea of the historical imagination and the idea of a universal science vied for it. But today – and on this we must bow to the pressure of the times – the idea of human survival, and of the most urgent threats to human survival, have become the proper and central preoccupation of those most privileged to enjoy the intellectual inheritance of mankind.

At the same time, however, Survival Studies could provide a much needed bridge between those who enjoy full-time higher education, and those who for one reason or another can never hope to do so. Survival Studies are, almost by definition, popular studies: and a general awareness that they are being pursued within universities and polytechnics would add greatly to the popularity of those institutions with the public at large. Our universities and polytechnics have every need of such support. They are currently under attack from a philistine government on the ground of the unpracticality of many of their courses of study. And no doubt there are political philistines who would have the audacity to accuse Survival Studies of unpracticality – or more specifically, of unprofitability. But although the public at large can swallow a great deal, I doubt if it would swallow this particular impertinence. Is it part of the task of government in a free society to discourage its ablest young people from thinking for themselves, and from informing themselves as fully as possible, on the condition of national and social survival?

These claims will of course be greeted in certain academic circles with hoots of derision. There will be the usual outcry against easy options which the ablest students will despise, and against the abandonment of those subjects which, by their remoteness or abstractness, virtually enforce habits of objectivity and impartiality. This is not the place to meet these charges in detail: it will be enough to indicate the head-on force of my main answer to them.

The outlook of our universities today, although vastly preferable to what its governmental critics would like it to be, is far from being as vigorous, confident and inspiring as it needs to be. This is due mainly, I believe, to a falling-off of the 'Newman effect' which I mentioned above, which is due in turn largely to the notorious separation – one could almost say the divorce – of 'the two cultures'. Instead of the clash *and support* of young minds of markedly different aptitudes and training, there is commonly found today, among university students and staffs alike, a hardly veiled intellectual indifference between those who see themselves as the expanders and those who feel themselves the conservers of our intellectual heritage. One way of overcoming this situation, which has been with us for the greater part of our century, would be the common engagement by all university students in some aspect of Survival Studies. This would help to engender what I have found, throughout my teaching life, so painfully missing in even the greatest of our universities: a sense of intellectual community, the sense of belonging to what Charles Peirce called 'the community of inquirers', which is today one of the two main hopes for the future of mankind. But in order to learn, to be astonished and to 'advance the boundaries of the accessible' one must *survive*. This simple thought must find an echo in the minds and hearts of many university teachers, students, as well as of countless others eager to follow in their lead. 'Why do you wait, dear friends?' – I translate freely from a great philosopher-poet – 'Rise up, the time is ripe.'

Index